The
Connell Guide
to
F. Scott Fitzgerald's

The Great Gatsby

by
John Sutherland &
Jolyon Connell

Contents

Introduction 4

A summary of the plot 6

What is *The Great Gatsby* about? 10

How important is the narrator in the novel? 21

How do Nick's shortcomings as a man affect the way he tells his tale? 28

How plausible is Gatsby? 35

Is Gatsby's dream always doomed? 45

The title 10

Why "Gatsby"? 14

Elegiac romance 19

Meet Mr Gatz 36

Six key quotes 44

What exactly is Gatsby's "racket"? 47

Gatsby believed in the green light 50

Meyer Wolfshiem/Arnold Rothstein 54

Newly rich 56

Fitzgerald and money 58

Great? 63

How much does money matter in the novel? 55

How does Gatsby compare with Tom? 63

What does *The Great Gatsby* tell us about the American Dream? 72

How does Fitzgerald treat women in the novel? 87

What does the novel tell us about the nature of dreams? 94

How great is *The Great Gatsby*? 104

Ten facts about The Great Gatsby *64*

Gatsby's heroic military career (or not) 76

Scott Fitzgerald's unheroic military career 78

Drink and remembrance of times past 97

Fitzgeraldian overwriting 107

How the novel was received 108

A brief biography 112

What the critics say... 119

A short chronology 120

Bibliography 122

Index 124

Introduction

When *The Great Gatsby* was first published, in 1925, reviews were mixed. H.L. Mencken called it "no more than a glorified anecdote". L.P. Hartley, author of *The Go-Between*, thought Fitzgerald deserved "a good shaking": "his imagination is febrile and his emotion over-strained... *The Great Gatsby* is evidently not a satire; but one would like to think that Mr Fitzgerald's heart is not in it, that it is a piece of mere naughtiness."

Yet gradually the book came to be seen as one of the greatest – if not *the* greatest – of American novels. Why? What is it that makes this story of a petty hoodlum so compelling? Why has a novel so intimately rooted in its own time "lasted" into ours? What is it that posterity, eight decades later, finds so fascinating in this chronicle of the long-gone "Jazz Age", flappers, speakeasies and wild parties?

It is, after all, scarcely a novel at all, more a long short story. But it has a power out of all proportion to its length. It is beautifully written, making it feel even shorter than it is, and is full of haunting imagery. It is also, perhaps, the most vivid literary evocation of the "Great American Dream", about which it is profoundly sceptical, as it is about dreams generally. In the end, however, as D.H. Lawrence would put it, it is "on the side of life".

Gatsby's dream may be impossible, so much so that the book can end in no other way than with his death, but up to a point he is redeemed by it and by the tenacity with which he clings to it. It is this that makes the novel so moving and so haunting.

The overwhelming majority of novels come, enjoy their brief moment, and go into oblivion never to return, but not this one. As George Orwell said, "Ultimately there is no test of literary merit except survival". As every bookshop and educational syllabus testifies, *The Great Gatsby* has survived.

A Summary of the Plot

Gatsby's story is narrated by Nick Carraway, a Midwesterner in his mid-twenties who has "come East". The story covers the summer of 1922 and is set mainly on the two spits of land off Long Island: East Egg and West Egg. West Egg, which is nearer New York, is populated by "new money", the more exclusive East Egg, by "old money".

Nick has taken a job as a bond salesman in Wall Street, where he commutes daily by train. He lives in a ramshackle "cardboard" house on West Egg adjoining "an elaborate road house", owned by the mysterious and very rich Mr Gatsby, who throws parties which, even for the Jazz Age, are extravagant. Rumours swirl around Gatsby: he is a gangster, a war hero, an aristocratic foreigner.

In another mansion – on more fashionable East Egg – lives Daisy Buchanan, a cousin of Nick's. Daisy is married to Tom, whose main interests in life are his polo ponies and his mistresses. Nick was a classmate of Tom's at Yale where he (Tom) was a star footballer. Now he is a bully, a snob, a racist and an inveterate adulterer. He and Daisy have come East after an ugly business involving a car accident and one of his "sweeties".

Tom has more recently found another sweetie in Myrtle, the coarse but sexually alluring wife of a local garage owner, George Wilson. Tom has set up a love-nest for her in Manhattan. Myrtle's husband suspects nothing. Daisy, however, knows about her husband's infidelities.

Before Tom married Daisy, we learn, she had been engaged to Jay Gatsby, then a young army officer. But Gatsby, after being sent to France, was delayed in Europe for several months after the war had ended – and during the delay, Daisy married Tom. Now Gatsby, who has felt spiritually "married" to Daisy ever since, has returned to New York to win her back.

Keeping Daisy company over the summer is her girlhood friend Jordan Baker – a champion golfer. She and Nick start an affair, which gives him an insight into the unfolding Buchanan-Gatsby drama as it moves towards its climax.

It is never really clear where Gatsby's immense riches come from, but gradually we learn more of his history. He was born Jimmy Gatz, the son of an unsuccessful farmer in the Midwest. Scraping a living on the shores of Lake Superior, young Gatz caught sight of a yacht in danger of being wrecked on a sandbar. He rowed out to warn the owner, Dan Cody. Cody, a "debauched" magnate enriched by his investments in metal mining, took to "Gatsby", as the young man promptly renamed himself. Over the next few years, he became Cody's right-hand man. More importantly, he learned how to look and act rich.

On Cody's death, Gatsby was left almost penniless, having inherited nothing from his former mentor, but contrived to get himself on an officer's training course, when America joined the war against Germany. It was as Lieutenant Gatsby that he won the heart of the southern belle, Daisy Fay.

After the war, having lost Daisy to Tom, Gatsby was taken up by another patron, the Jewish gangster, Meyer Wolfshiem, and became involved in the racketeering that boomed in the Prohibition era (1919-33): fixing sports events, rum-running, running illicit casinos, speakeasies and brothels, dealing in stolen bonds, even – it is rumoured – murder. We are uneasily aware of all this as a "foul dust", trailing the dazzling Gatsby glamour.

By 1922, Gatsby is rich enough to pursue his dream of reclaiming Daisy and the main narrative of Fitzgerald's novel revolves around a series of summer parties, lavish (in Gatsby's West Egg mansion) and squalid (in Tom's New York love nest).

There is a final showdown between Gatsby and Daisy's husband, Tom, in the Manhattan Plaza Hotel. Gatsby declares his intention to run off with Daisy. She is present, as are Nick and Jordan, and cannot decisively say which man she loves. After this tense encounter, Gatsby and

Daisy drive back to Long Island together. She is driving, allegedly "to steady her nerves".

As they pass George Wilson's garage, Myrtle contrives to break out from the bedroom where her husband (suspicious at last) has locked her. The unlucky woman assumes Tom is in the speeding car, rushes into the road, and is killed. Daisy, terrified, drives on. The police are later unable to identify the "death car".

Gallantly, Gatsby does not reveal that Daisy was the driver. Tom tells Wilson it was Gatsby, and Wilson, in a fit of homicidal rage, guns down Gatsby in his swimming pool before shooting himself. Nick knows the truth about the hit and run incident but keeps it to himself. The Buchanans "retreat into their money". Nick returns to his home in the Midwest.

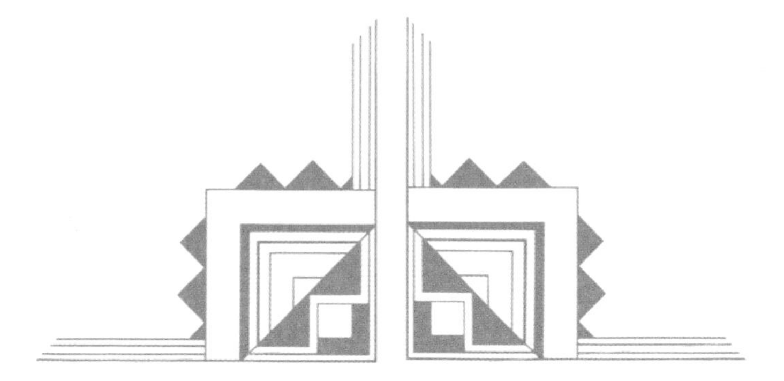

What is *The Great Gatsby* about?

The Great Gatsby is a young man's novel – a novel about being young, and about the loss of youthful dreams.

No-one, Fitzgerald proclaimed, after the triumph of his first book, *This Side of Paradise*, should live beyond the age of 30. That novel was published when he was a precocious 23. *The Great Gatsby* is another novel about the 1920s, written by a novelist still in his twenties. It has a narrator in his twenties and a hero only a year past them attempting to recover the woman he loved when he was 27. Our twenties are not only the best time in our lives, *The Great Gatsby*

THE TITLE

Few novelists have entitled their work more poetically, or more aptly, than F. Scott Fitzgerald. Finding the "right" title for his third novel, however, caused chronic problems for the author and his faithful editor, Maxwell Perkins.

The Great Gatsby was, the manuscript workings reveal, an early title, soon discarded. Fitzgerald initially disliked it. As he told Perkins "*The Great Gatsby* is weak because there's no emphasis, even ironically, on [Gatsby's] greatness or lack of it".

Other titles the two men kicked around between them were: *Among*

asserts. They are the only worthwhile time in our lives.

The novelist Jacqueline Susann once observed that "for every woman, forty is Hiroshima". Fitzgerald was even more apocalyptic. In his world, thirty is the "far side of paradise". The point is stressed when, late in the novel, driving back with Tom from New York, Nick Carraway, the narrator, suddenly realises that it's his birthday. He has passed, without realising it, what Joseph Conrad called the "shadow line" in his life. Darkness awaits:

> *I was thirty. Before me stretched the portentous, menacing road of a new decade... Thirty – the promise of a decade of loneliness, a thinning list of single men to know, a thinning brief-case of*

---

the Ash Heaps and Millionaires (Perkins thought the stress on "Ash" would put readers off); *Gold-hatted Gatsby* (grotesque in the image it evokes); *Trimalchio in West Egg* (as Fitzgerald's friend Ring Lardner pointed out, no-one would know how to pronounce Trimalchio, or know who the hell he was – or, come to that, what kind of hen laid west eggs); *On the Road to West Egg*; *The High-bouncing Lover*, or, pure and simple, *Gatsby*.

Fitzgerald's last brainwave, communicated to Perkins by telegram – after the novel had gone to press – was *The Red White and Blue* (alluding to the *Star-Spangled Banner*, composed by Fitzgerald's distant relative, Francis Scott Key).

Perkins eventually persuaded his author to go with *The Great Gatsby*.

*enthusiasm, thinning hair... So we drove on toward death through the cooling twilight. (7)**

As the critic Matthew Bruccoli has observed, the primary emotion *The Great Gatsby* generates is regret: regret for the loss of youth and of youthful dreams and "for depleted emotional capacity, a regret as intense as the emotions that inspired it were".

While writing *The Great Gatsby*, Fitzgerald acknowledged that this was indeed his intention in a letter to a friend:

> That's the whole burden of the novel – the loss of those illusions that give such color to the world that you don't care whether things are true or false as long as they partake of the magical glory.

But if *The Great Gatsby* is about a particular time of life, it is as much about a particular era in American history. Set in 1922, it is *the* novel about what became known as the Jazz Age (a term, incidentally, which Fitzgerald himself invented).

Fitzgerald, of course, was not a documentary writer and his grasp of historical detail is occasionally shaky. He took little interest in politics or the stock market and knew little about organised crime. Nonetheless, no writer has caught the "feel" of the

* Throughout this book, the numbers in brackets refer to the chapters from which quotes are taken

"Roaring Twenties" better, and *The Great Gatsby* is as damning an indictment of a civilisation in decay without ever having fully flowered as anything to be found in American literature. Gatsby represents America; his youthful dream is America's; his loss is America's loss. The novel mourns the death of the American Dream while simultaneously mourning the passing of youth.

In 1931, in an article about the Jazz Age, Fitzgerald talked of a generation living on "borrowed time" and of the "whole upper tenth" of the country "living with the insouciance of grand dukes or casualness of chorus girls". A few years later, in an essay reflecting ruefully on his early success, he expanded on this theme:

> The uncertainties of 1919 were over – there seemed little doubt about what was going to happen – America was going on the greatest, gaudiest spree in history and there was going to be plenty to tell about it. The whole golden boom was in the air – its splendid generosities, its outrageous corruptions and the tortuous death struggle of the old America in Prohibition. All the stories that came into my head had a touch of disaster in them – the lovely creatures in my novels went to ruin, the diamond mountains of my short stories blew up, my millionaires were as beautiful and damned as Thomas Hardy's peasants.

Fitzgerald was writing in *The Great Gatsby* about a world turned upside down by the First World War – a world infused with a collective sense of disillusionment and despair at the loss of settled values. The writer Gertrude Stein described young adults after the war as "a lost generation of men and women adrift in a chaotic hell of their own solipsism".

Bereft of beliefs, they lived for thrills. This idea of people in continuous frenetic pursuit of hedonistic excitement features in other novels of the period, notably those of Fitzgerald's near contemporary, and closest literary friend, Ernest Hemingway – although in Hemingway's case they tended to be people living the expatriate life (as Daisy and Tom, in *The Great Gatsby*, also do for a while).

This, then, is the mood which Fitzgerald creates.

WHY "GATSBY"?

James Gatz invents his name, we are told, on his first encounter with the metal magnate, Dan Cody. It's chosen for its English resonance – like "Ponsonby" or "Willoughby", "Gatsby" has a classy "Waspy" feel to it. It seems clear that Fitzgerald picked the name up from a short story of that most English of writers, Rudyard Kipling. In Kipling's "The Story of the Gadsbys", Captain Gadsby is a cavalryman in the "Pink Hussars" (Gatsby is also a captain, and wears a pink suit) and is given to slang of the "old sport" kind.

If the Jeffersonian dream of a peace-loving, unmaterialistic America of infinite potential had not died before America's involvement in the horrors of the First World War, *The Great Gatsby* implies, it died in the mud of Flanders.

The theme of *The Great Gatsby* was prefigured in a short story Fitzgerald wrote in 1922, not long before he began serious work on the novel. In "Winter Dreams", the hero is a poor young man who becomes unexpectedly wealthy but loses the girl of his dreams. As a boy he was a caddy and later, when he becomes rich and has caddies of his own, he keeps looking at them, "trying to catch a gleam or gesture that would remind him of himself, that would lessen the gap which lay between his present and his past".

Green, like Jay Gatsby, is haunted not just by his dreams but by the loss of his younger self. He sees his future as lying in the past – and when, at the end, he learns that the beauty of the girl he loves has faded, he experiences a poignant yearning, like Gatsby, for what he has forever lost:

> *The dream was gone. Something had been taken from him. In a sort of panic he pushed the palms of his hands into his eyes and tried to bring up a picture of the waters lapping on Sherry Island and the moonlit veranda, and gingham on the golf-links and the dry sun and the gold colour of her neck's soft down. And her mouth clamped to his kisses and her eyes plaintive with melancholy*

The GREAT GATSBY
F·SCOTT·FITZGERALD

and her freshness like new fine linen in the morning. Why, these things were no longer in the world! They had existed, and they existed no longer.

For the first time the tears were streaming down his face. But they were for himself now. He did not care about mouth and eyes and moving hands. He wanted to care but could not care. For he had gone away and he could never come back any more. The gates were closed, the sun was gone down, and there was no beauty but the gay beauty of steel that withstands all time. Even the grief he could have borne was left behind in the country of illusions, of youth, of the richness of life, when his winter dreams had flourished.

"Long ago," he said, "long ago, there was something in me, but now that thing is gone. Now that thing is gone, that thing is gone. I cannot cry. I cannot care. That thing will come back no more."

But while Green grieves for what has gone, and the fact that he can no longer respond to "the richness of life", he doesn't fight the sensation. Gatsby does:

"'Can't repeat to the past?' he cried incredulously. 'Why of course you can!'" (6)

And in a novel full of very unheroic characters – including the narrator, Nick Carraway – there is

opposite: the original cover of the book, 1925

something heroic, the book suggests, in Gatsby's attempt to recapture his dream.

The sense of loss, and of time inexorably passing, is reinforced in *The Great Gatsby* by a profusion of references to time: there are, it has been calculated, a total of 450 time words in the novel, words like *moment, minute, day, year, month, past, clock*, etc. The critic Malcolm Cowley once observed that Fitzgerald wrote as if surrounded by clocks and calendars.

The sense of time passing is woven into the fabric of the narrative. In the middle of the novel, when Gatsby is reunited with Daisy, his head "leaned back so far that it rested against the face of a defunct mantelpiece clock" (5). A moment later he nearly knocks it off the mantelpiece, "whereupon he turned and caught it with trembling fingers, and set it back in place". It is a strikingly ironic image: the clock may have stopped but nothing can stop time. "We're getting old," sighs Daisy at the last party in New York, when they hear the sound of a jazz band and think that, had they been younger, they would have got up and danced.

Before settling on *The Great Gatsby* as the title, Fitzgerald toyed with other possibilities. His original plan had been to call it *Trimalchio in West Egg*, Trimalchio being a vulgar and rich social upstart in Petronius's *Satyricon*, a man who loves giving banquets as Gatsby loves giving parties. Trimalchio is also, like Gatsby, acutely conscious of time passing and is described by one of his guests as "a very rich man, who has a clock and a uniformed trumpeter in his dining room, to keep telling him how much of his life is lost and gone". But there is one important difference between the two men: Gatsby, unlike Trimalchio, treats his parties as a spectacle and doesn't participate in them.

At the heart of *The Great Gatsby* is a paradox: only in youth, Fitzgerald suggests, can we have truly intense experiences, can we feel truly abandoned to the moment. Yet this sense of abandonment can be so intense as to submerge any consciousness of

ELEGIAC ROMANCE

Kenneth Bruffee regards *The Great Gatsby* as an elegiac romance – that is, a modern, anti-heroic form of "quest romance". He sees the evolution of the quest romance as being divided into four phases:

1. The first of these is the courtly phase of *Sir Gawain and the Green Knight* and *Parzival*, when our attention is entirely on the "task and character of the aristocratic seeker, the knight". The knight's goal is to overcome weaknesses in his own character so he can deserve his reputation for chivalric gallantry.

2. In the hands of Cervantes, this changes – and the story becomes ironic. No longer is our attention exclusively on the knight (Don Quixote); it is just as much on his squire (Sancho Panza), and the reader "is never allowed to

enjoyment, and the attempt to live the moment to the full later is doomed because by then it is too late – too late for new, similar experiences, because youth is gone, and too late to recapture the experiences of youth or even how it felt to have those experiences. As Susan Parr has put it, except in the imagination "the past is irrecoverable" while "the present brings with it only the betrayal of dreams".

In *This Side of Paradise*, Fitzgerald made this point in a slightly different way: "The sentimental person thinks things will last – the romantic person has a desperate confidence they won't." Fitzgerald was conscious of the danger of holding

---

feel quite sure whose values Cervantes means him to share: the knight's or the squire's". For the first time, the conventions and values of feudal life, courtly love etc, are held up for criticism in the light of everyday experience. There is an ambivalence: Sancho begins by thinking Don Quixote stupid but eventually falls in love with his master's madness.

3. In the third, Romantic phase, the pendulum swings away from the knight's quest towards the "everyday experience, needs, and interests of the squire". In this phase, like the first, there is no irony. This is the age when "feudal values, in the form of aristocratic political hegemony, are flatly rejected", the age of the French Revolution when, in Wordsworth's words, it is bliss to be alive, and to be young is very heaven. The "quest romance" is now internalised; the Romantic preoccupation is with self, with personal growth. The attention now is on the

on to our dreams for too long, and it is the potentially devastating consequence of doing this, and of trying to make them the basis for action, which he dramatises so effectively in *The Great Gatsby*.

How important is the narrator in the novel?

The narrative frame of *The Great Gatsby* clearly derives from another short novel, Joseph Conrad's *Heart of Darkness*. Fitzgerald hugely admired Conrad,

---

squire not on the knight; the truth-seeking, Romantic "I" becomes the hero.

4. The fourth phase, to which *The Great Gatsby* belongs, is the phase of what Bruffee calls elegiac romance. In this phase, the quest romance becomes the story "of its own failure", and here, once again, there is irony. As in Cervantes, it may be unclear at first whose values we are meant to share. The knights of elegiac romance are early 20th century figures like Kurtz in *Heat of Darkness* and Jim in *Lord Jim*, Edward Ashburnham in Ford Madox Ford's *The Good Soldier*, Vladimir Nabokov's Sebastian Knight and Gatsby. They are "obsessed by the goal of their quest", just as Gawain and Parzival were. The squires of elegiac romance – i.e. the narrators like Nick – have in some sense, like Sancho Panza, fallen in love with their master's madness. But they recognise that it is a kind of madness. In elegiac romance the knight doesn't change or mellow or develop: the

who died while he was at work on *The Great Gatsby*. (Fitzgerald was profoundly affected by the event.) He was particularly influenced by the way in which Conrad manipulates time, so that we discover things bit by bit, as we do in life, by his rich and evocative imagery and, in particular, by his use of an observing narrator to tell his story.

Marlow in *Heart of Darkness*, though appalled by the adventurer Kurtz's deplorable behaviour in the Belgian Congo, is fascinated by him and comes, in the end, despite his awfulness, to see him as more real than those who've stayed

only important change he undergoes is that he dies. Elegiac romance, in short, is an attempt to dispense with conventional heroes and old-fashioned notions of heroism. What matters is "the enlightenment of the squire-narrator".

The narrator tries to "seduce the reader into sharing first his illusion and then his disillusionment", says Bruffee, so that the reader will not just "respond" but gain a sort of self-knowledge in the process. "In elegiac romance, the quest of the squire-narrator is our quest."

Bruffee sums up the ingredients:

> The *necessary conditions...* are the narrator's protracted hero worship of his friend and his friend's death, before the narrator begins to tell the tale. The *occasion* of the narrator's tale is his irretrievable loss of his hero. The *ostensible purpose* of his tale is to memorialise his lost hero. The *real purpose* of his tale is to recover the coherence of his own interior world, lost when he lost the screen, so to speak, upon which he had projected his fantasies.

safely behind in Europe. Gatsby comes to acquire similar heroic status for Nick Carraway, the narrator of *The Great Gatsby*, though Nick is perfectly conscious, as was Marlow, that he is morally compromised by his hero-worship.

The opening paragraphs of *The Great Gatsby* are very brilliant in establishing Nick's character and interest. His voice recalls Marlow's and is impressive in some of the same engagingly wry ways. He tells us, for example, that "Reserving judgement is a matter of infinite hope", before coming "to the admission that it has a limit": "Conduct may be founded on the hard rock or the wet marshes but after a certain point I don't care what it's founded on."* (1)

Like Marlow, Nick is concerned with "conduct" in a way that shows his probity, and what he says in these early paragraphs is borne out by events. Gatsby, it becomes clear, is involved in selling bonds in some corrupt or criminal way, and when, in Chapter Five, he suddenly offers Nick a way into this easy dirty money, Nick – who is in this

* This is very like Marlow when, in *Lord Jim*, he says that Jim felt the "demand of some such truth or some such illusion" before adding: "I don't care how you call it, there is so little difference, and the difference means so little." One might compare, too, Marlow's snappily devastating response when Jim pleads that "there was not the thickness of a sheet of paper between the right and the wrong of this affair: 'How much more did you want?'"

important if limited sense genuinely "honest" – recoils. Later, near the end of the novel, Nick takes a phone call from a man who mistakes him for Gatsby. The call shows that the police have caught up with the bond racket, but Nick, to his great credit, doesn't allow himself a self-congratulatory reflection on how lucky he was not to get mixed up in it himself.*

The voice we hear in the opening pages of *The Great Gatsby* is subtle and compelling: it holds our attention and wins our respect more than any other we hear in the novel. When Fitzgerald's clever editor, Maxwell Perkins, read the manuscript, he thought Chapters Six and Seven were the weakest; Fitzgerald himself had also decided (before reading Perkins's reader's report) that they were "shaky". This may seem odd in a way, because they are the chapters which bring the novel to its climax – the hit-and-run car accident which leads to the final catastrophe – so they ought to be more gripping than they are.

But it isn't really odd at all, since we hear little from Nick in these chapters. The voices we hear instead are those of the other characters, who are more vacuous and one-dimensional than he is.

* Had he lived to read the novel, it is likely that Conrad, whose interest in "sustaining illusions" was closely aligned with his "work ethic", would have noticed this and been impressed by the way Fitzgerald handles it.

opposite: Joseph Conrad

Arguably, with Nick so much in the background, it is harder to sustain an interest in their world – to care about what happens *to* them when nothing really happens *in* them. Gatsby, after all, is never explained as a character; nor, in *Heart of Darkness*, is Kurtz: what chiefly interests us about both of them is the effect they have on the narrators, which is precisely because in these two cases the narrators are also the real protagonists.*

There are echoes of *Heart of Darkness* throughout *The Great Gatsby*. Nick's last tribute to Gatsby, for example, recalls the key moment in *Heart of Darkness* in which Marlow delivers his epitaph on Kurtz – the mad, genocidal, plunderer of the upper Congo's ivory wealth. Kurtz was, Marlow "affirms", despite all his loathsome crimes against black humanity, "a remarkable man". Why? Because he had looked over the edge of life into the "Heart of Darkness", and had taken the plummeting final step:

> *Since I had peeped over the edge myself, I understand better the meaning of his stare, that could not see the flame of the candle, but was wide enough to embrace the whole universe, piercing*

* This is not true of Marlow in *Lord Jim*: in *Lord Jim* it is Jim, a more complex figure than either Kurtz or Gatsby, who is the hero, or anti-hero.

enough to penetrate all the hearts that beat in the darkness. It was an affirmation, a moral victory paid for by innumerable defeats, by abominable terrors, by abominable satisfactions... But it was a victory! That is why I have remained loyal to Kurtz to the last.

Kenneth Bruffee has described *The Great Gatsby* as an "elegiac romance" (see p.19), arguing that our real interest is always in the narrator and not in the book's actual hero. This is true of Marlow, as in the passage above, and it is true of Nick:

> We never see the hero "as he was". We never know for sure what he was "really" like, what he "really" did, or what "really" happened to him. We must take the narrator's account of the hero, even his very existence, on faith... [It] is axiomatic of elegiac romance that the narrator's hero exists, as Marlow says of Jim, "for me, and after all it is only through me that he exists for you".

The implication of this is that, to understand the stories these narrators are telling, we need, most of all, to understand them, and to understand, too, why they are telling us their stories at all.

How do Nick's shortcomings as a man man affect the way he tells his tale?

Conrad was preoccupied with the question: what do men live *for*? He was fascinated by how illusions shape our lives and how fragile they are: the notion that "human kind/Cannot bear very much reality" – in T.S. Eliot's phrase from *Four Quartets* – runs through all Conrad's work. It runs through *The Great Gatsby*, too, a novel which is centrally concerned with illusions – with Nick's illusions as much as with Gatsby's.

This matters a lot, because Nick is flawed, and while his judgements are often acute – he is, as it were, the "fine conscience" of the novel – his shortcomings as a man crucially affect the way he tells the story.

Tony Tanner, in his introduction to the Penguin edition of *The Great Gatsby*, describes Nick, who is much younger and less "knowing" than Marlow, as "a spectator in search of a performer" and goes on to compare him to the emotionally timid Lockwood putting together his narrative account of Heathcliff in *Wuthering Heights*. Nick has slid out of an engagement in the Midwest before coming East, and in New York he has "a short affair with a girl who lived in Jersey City and worked in the accounting department" (3). But her brother throws "mean looks" in his direction and, typically, he lets the relationship "blow away", just as he later lets Jordan Baker "blow away" too.

"I was conscious of wanting to look squarely at everyone, and yet to avoid all eyes" (1), he says. Like Henry James's sexually fearful Isabel Archer in *The Portrait of a Lady,* he wants "to see but not to feel". When it comes to the erotic, life in fantasy is "safer" than real life:

> *I liked to walk up Fifth Avenue and pick out romantic women from the crowd and imagine that in a few minutes I was going to enter into their lives, and no-one would ever know or disapprove. Sometimes, in my mind, I followed them to their apartments on the corners of hidden streets, and they turned and smiled back at me before they faded through a door into warm darkness. (3)*

In a passage that, like many in the novel, echoes Eliot's *The Waste Land,* Nick goes on to say:

> *At the enchanted metropolitan twilight I felt a haunting loneliness sometimes, and felt it in others – poor young clerks who loitered in front of windows waiting until it was time for a solitary restaurant dinner – young clerks in the dusk, wasting the most*

poignant moments of night and life. * *(3)*

Life on the sidelines is where Nick Carraway is happiest. Essentially passive, he is no match for the brutish Tom, who, when he drives him to New York, almost manhandles him into his girlfriend's house – "he literally forced me from the car". His determination to have my company "bordered on violence", says Nick, though he has nothing better to do so he goes along anyway. Then he doesn't want to go to Myrtle's apartment and tries to leave but Tom prevents this:

> *"No, you don't," interposed Tom quickly. "Myrtle'll be hurt if you don't come up to the apartment. Won't you, Myrtle?"* *(2)*

Once in her flat, Nick's instinct is to "pull out" but, despite himself, he keeps getting "entangled" and "pulled back":

> *Yet high over the city our line of yellow windows must have contributed their share of human secrecy to the casual watcher in the darkening streets, and I saw him [Gatsby] too, looking up and wondering. I was within and without, simultaneously enchanted and repelled by the*

* The inscription in the copy of *The Great Gatsby* Fitzgerald sent to Eliot read: "To the greatest of living poets from his enthusiastic worshipper."

inexhaustible variety of life. (2)

Whether conscious of it or not, Nick is here echoing Walt Whitman, almost directly ("in and out of the game, watching and wondering at it"). It is clear that his preferred role in the drama is to be that of the "casual watcher".

Although he drifts into a relationship with Jordan Baker, his heart is never in the affair. He says early on that he would like "the world to be in uniform and at a sort of moral attention forever" (1) and seems to be attracted to Jordan Baker partly because, unlike him, she knows exactly what she wants from life – a quality she shares with Gatsby – and partly because he values order and stability: with her male-like body ("slender and small-breasted"), he says, she looked like "a young cadet".

Jordan, for her part, likes him because she says that, unlike her, he is a "careful driver". In a similar metaphor, Nick himself confesses to being "slow-thinking and full of interior rules that act as brakes on my desires".

In keeping with his character, he explains his decision to break from Jordan in housekeeping terms: "I wanted to leave things in order and not just trust that obliging and indifferent sea to sweep my refuse away." (9) At the first, drunken party in New York, he fastidiously wipes a spot of "dried lather" (2) off the cheek of a man asleep in a chair – a gesture which looks even more futile immediately afterwards when Tom breaks Myrtle's nose and there is blood all over the carpet.

And when, at the end of the story, Nick returns to have a final look at Gatsby's "huge incoherent failure of a house", he sees, scrawled on the white steps, "an obscene word, scrawled by some boy with a piece of brick", standing out in the moonlight. True to his instinct for tidiness, he rubs it out, "drawing my shoe raspingly along the stone".

For all his qualms about Gatsby's behaviour, Nick tries to ignore or erase whatever makes his idol appear in a less flattering light. It is part of Fitzgerald's skill in handling the narrative that he constantly, but tactfully, alerts us (through Nick as the narrator) to shadier details in Gatsby's past, while at the same time showing us how Nick tries to make light of them – and why. In the same way, Nick thinks of Gatsby's early relationship with Daisy in purely romantic terms, learning only later that when he first made love to her he took her "ravenously and unscrupulously".

Nick's reluctance to acknowledge the seamier side of reality is evident when he first drives out to the valley of ashes and sees the "dim garage" with a "dust-covered wreck of a Ford... crouched" in front of it. His instinct is that "this shadow of a garage must be a blind, and that sumptuous and romantic apartments were concealed overhead..." It is typical of the way Nick thinks.

He is frequently embellishing the truth. When Gatsby says of Daisy that her voice "is full of money", for example, it sets him off into a fantasy about Daisy as a princess when in fact all Gatsby meant, quite clearly, was that she came from a background of "old money". Nick records what he sees but he never quite engages with life and is always dreaming. Tony Tanner wonders: "Is the whole work the self-consoling hanky-panky of a miserable failure of a bachelor, who invents a 'gorgeous' figure to compensate for the 'dismal' Middle West which he has fled and to which he eventually returns?"

The truth about Nick is that he is a hollow man – a vacuum – and the judgement of a hollow man is always suspect. Nothing makes a lasting impression on him. He has no real convictions. He says he is "one of the few honest people that I have ever known" (3) and while this may be literally true – in the limited sense that he is incapable of villainy – he is a dreamer; honesty is an easy virtue to claim, and there is a vast gulf, the novel suggests, between honesty, as Nick conceives it, and integrity. He lets relationships "blow away" and, being weak, is easily pushed around by Tom and Jordan and, indeed, Gatsby. Even at the end of the book he is protesting that he has always disapproved of his hero but at the same time he comes close to worshipping him without any apparent awareness of the contradiction.

Nick lives his life vicariously; his involvement

with Gatsby is a kind of displacement activity. The book he writes is a voyeur's book, and in the writing of it and the words he uses, he is trying to comfort himself. Conrad saw the use of words as simply another way of escaping reality. "Words also belong to the sheltering conception of light and order which is our refuge," as Marlow puts it in *Lord Jim*. The most honest man is the man of fewest words.

But while Nick is a miserable failure, so too is Gatsby. Both of them try to escape what is "dismal" in their surroundings. Both suffer from arrested development, neither wishing to make the leap from childhood to adulthood, preferring instead to hold on to their dreams.

How plausible is Gatsby?

From the beginning, Gatsby is wrapped in an aura of mystery and intrigue – an effect cleverly contrived, through the narrator, by Fitzgerald. Gatsby is perennially elusive. He flits through the narrative like an image in a hall of mirrors – brilliantly vivid, but superficial and fleeting.

One of the most striking things about Gatsby is his solitariness. His first appearance, at the end of Chapter One, is appropriately spectral. Nick has wandered on to his lawn, which is next door to Gatsby's, for a minute or two's contemplation before turning in. It is the witching hour:

> *The wind had blown off, leaving a loud, bright night, with wings beating in the trees and a persistent organ sound as the full bellows of the earth blew the frogs full of life. The silhouette of a moving cat wavered across the moonlight, and, turning my head to watch it, I saw that I was not alone – fifty feet away a figure had emerged from the shadow of my neighbour's mansion and was standing with his hands in his pockets regarding the silver pepper of the stars. Something in his leisurely movements and the secure position of his feet upon the lawn suggested that it was Mr Gatsby himself, come out to determine what share was his of our local heavens. (1)*

opposite: Robert Redford as Jay Gatsby in the 1974 film

It is a highly romantic image, with the moonlight and the stars, and it conveys both Gatsby's sense of unreality and how Nick, from the beginning, romanticises him. For Gatsby is not "real". He has made himself up. His life is a fabrication, built on make-believe and denial of his origins. At the age of 17, he defined for himself a completely new identity, turning his back on his past. As Nick puts it: "The truth was that Jay Gatsby of West Egg, Long Island, sprang from his platonic conception of himself." (6)

The boy born Jimmy Gatz blamed his parents for his unhappiness. In his imagination, he "had never really accepted them as his parents at all". The idea

MEET MR GATZ

It isn't until half-way through the narrative that we get any clear pedigree of the hero. The first account of his background which Gatsby supplies Nick is suspiciously "creative". He's from the mid-West, Gatsby says – going on to specify "San Francisco" which is, of course, as far west as you can go without getting very wet. Forget "mid". He was educated at Oxford. His family, he says, all died and he came into a lot of money:

> "After that I lived like a young rajah in all the capitals of Europe – Paris, Venice, Rome – collecting jewels, chiefly rubies, hunting big game, painting a little, things for myself only, and trying to forget something very sad that happened to me long ago." (4)

As Nick sardonically replies, the Bois de

of rejecting or denying one's parents, while not uniquely American – Freud, after all, identifies it as a common human impulse in "Family Romances" – is quintessentially part of the New World fantasy. In a famous essay in 1836, the American essayist, philosopher and poet Ralph Waldo Emerson argued that fathers (and fathering countries, like England) should be forgotten. What mattered was self-reliance and self-invention:

> Why should we not also enjoy an original relation to the universe?... The sun shines today also... There are new lands, new men, new thoughts...

Boulogne does not exactly teem with tiger. Later, a more accurate CV is divulged, and very bleak it is. The "Great Gatsby" is, by birth: "James Gatz of North Dakota ... His parents were shiftless and unsuccessful farm people" (6). His father (the only parent to feature in this singularly parentless novel) makes a shabby appearance at his son's funeral. He once beat "Jimmy", we learn, for saying that he (his father) "'et like a pig".

What is one to make – genetically – of the Gatsby = Gatz information? From the invaluable website, www.ancestry.com, one discovers that American families with the surname "Gatz" were concentrated, as the national 1920 census reports, around Minnesota and Dakota (none, however, were registered in San Francisco). The name, the same website suggests, is most commonly an Americanisation of the Ukrainian and Polish "Gac". Not Nordic. Nor WASP, even (Jimmy Gatz doesn't qualify under the "Anglo-Saxon" provision).

But, conceivably, "Gatz" is not even Slavic. There is lively discussion on the

This notion of rootlessness is ever-present in *The Great Gatsby*. Fitzgerald's characters, like Conrad's, live outside the protective, insulated world of family relationships – they are metaphorically, if not literally, orphans. Nick repeatedly stresses how alone Gatsby is. He is alone when he is first encountered, gazing at the stars in Chapter One. At his party in Chapter Three, when girls are "swooning backward playfully into men's arms" and putting their heads on men's shoulders, no one swoons backward on Gatsby or puts their head on his shoulder.

At the end of the party Nick is struck by the "sudden emptiness" that seemed to flow from the

web (google "Gatz" + "Jewish" if you're curious) as to whether the hero's birth name is gentile at all, or whether it might more likely be a version of the Jewish "Getz" (as in the famous tenor saxophone player, Stan Getz). If, as is widely hypothesised, "Jay" (a common Jewish abbreviation for "Jacob") is Jewish, it would go a long way to explaining why the bootlegger Meyer Wolfshiem not merely befriends Gatsby, but actually makes him his heir apparent, enriching the young man beyond the dreams of avarice in three short years. Why would he throw his money at a gentile kid?

On the extremer fringes of blogosphere, and in some of the wilder academic conferences, it is suggested there may even be African-American blood coursing through the Gatsby veins - which, surely, is a speculation too far. The point is, Fitzgerald never supplies us the facial image against which we can check these racial stereotypes. Look, and you see only a blur.

windows and by the "complete isolation" of the party's host, standing on the porch with his hand raised "in a formal gesture of farewell". When Tom arrives at Gatsby's house in Chapter Six, with Mr Sloane and his wife, the Sloanes invite him to supper but don't actually want him to come, and escape before he has a chance to accept.

Early in the novel, Nick drives to New York with Gatsby and "A dead man passed us in a hearse heaped with blooms, followed by two carriages with drawn blinds and by more cheerful friends." (4) It is a telling image. Later, Nick can't find anyone to come to Gatsby's funeral and even Klipspringer, who had been living in a room at Gatsby's house, rings up and says he can't come because he will be at a picnic. (His reason for ringing up is equally trivial: he has left some tennis shoes at the house which he wants to collect.) Wolfshiem, Gatsby's underworld contact, won't come either, even though as Nick tells him: "You were his closest friend."

Only Owl Eyes, the bespectacled guest at Gatsby's first party, arrives to join Nick in the blessing of the dead and to add a 1920s benediction: "The poor son-of-a-bitch." It is the nearest thing to compassion expressed in the book, and, as Kathleen Parkinson says, it is interesting that it should come from a minor character, "an absurd figure" from Gatsby's parties.

This isolation is the price Gatsby pays for living his dream. It cuts him off from other people. ("One dies, as one dreams, alone," says Marlow in *Heart of Darkness.*) The extent to which Gatsby lives his dream and dies for it is evident towards the end, when Nick imagines Gatsby's state of mind after the accident and the way everything has changed:

> *He must have looked up at an unfamiliar sky through frightening leaves and shivered as he found what a grotesque thing a rose is and how raw the sunlight was upon the scarcely created grass. A new world, material without being real, where poor ghosts, breathing dreams like air, drifted fortuitously about... like that ashen, fantastic figure gliding towards him through the amorphous trees. (8)*

Now that Gatsby has lost his dream even the roses have become "grotesque" and the sunlight "raw". The passage, with its echoes of Plato, underlines the completeness with which he has reinvented himself.

Everything about Gatsby, after all, is contrived. Even his preposterous name has been carefully chosen to conceal his past and give him a touch of old-world glamour. Conrad also made great play of the hollowness of names and many of his characters are ironically titled: Baron Heyst, Gentleman Brown, Lord Jim, Capataz de Cargadores. He saw names as representative of the way in which human beings try to persuade themselves that they are solid and consistent. In Fitzgerald's book, the name Gatsby, with its ironic addition, Great – the name, as has been pointed out, making him sound like a cross between a conjuror and a superman – is also central to Jimmy Gatz's reinvention of himself, and, having adopted it, he also adopts what he believes are the appropriate mannerisms and surrounds himself with what he takes to be the right props. He calls other men "old sport", drives a fancy limousine and lives in a mansion in West Egg.

Gatsby has a flamboyant wardrobe which, significantly, is described in much more detail than his physiognomy. When Nick first sets eyes on him he is wearing a "caramel coloured suit". In Chapter Five he enters brilliantly attired in a "white flannel suit, silver shirt, and gold-coloured tie". In the climactic section of the novel he wears "a luminous pink suit" (somewhat bedraggled after the car accident and what follows). He orders new shirts every month from the best British shirtmakers. Their thick silk, sheer linen and fine flannel glory entrance Daisy.

Essentially the clothes, like everything else about Gatsby, imply unreality. "I hold that man to be well dressed," said Anthony Trollope, "whose dress nobody notices". This is not something which could ever be said about Gatsby, who always dresses for effect.

"I was crazy about *The Great Gatsby*. Old Gatsby.

Old sport. That killed me." So says Holden Caulfield in *The Catcher in the Rye*. He goes on to pay Gatsby the highest compliment in the Caulfield moral lexicon – he is not a "phony".

But of course he *is* a phony; indeed there is no-one phonier than Jimmy Gatz in the annals of American fiction. And there is no term of address phonier than "old sport". No farm-kid, scratching a living in the Midwest at the turn of the century, would have used such a clubby term of address. It rings false every time Gatsby uses it in the narrative.

Fitzgerald intended it to. Gatsby's transformation of himself, with his West Egg mansion and fancy car and chummy language, is as comprehensive as he can make it. Matthew Bruccoli points out that the earliest manuscript version of *The Great Gatsby* has "only four appearances of 'old sport'". It was in the second, revised, version that it was inserted all over the place, replacing Gatsby's less jarring "old fellow" and "old man".

Equally fake is his library. During the summer party described in Chapter Three, one of the guests, a "stout, middle-aged man with enormous owl-eyed spectacles" retires to the mansion's deserted library. He has been drunk for a week. Books, he quaintly thinks, might sober him up.

Nick finds Owl Eyes thoughtfully pondering the bookshelves. Turning on Nick and Jordan, he asks, "What do you think?" "The books?" inquires Nick, politely. Owl Eyes nods, explaining:

> *"Absolutely real – have pages and everything. I thought they'd be a nice durable cardboard. Matter of fact, they're absolutely real." (3)*

But Gatsby doesn't read books. The only book we know him ever to have read is *Hopalong Cassidy*, in whose dog-eared covers he inscribed his juvenile good intentions ("bath every two days" etc). One of those resolutions was, "Read one improving book or magazine a week" (9).

But the fakery is done with typical attention to detail. He has packed his shelves with expensive imitations, as Owl Eyes notices when he picks a volume randomly from the shelf:

> *"See ... It's a bona fide piece of printed matter. It fooled me. This fellow's a regular Belasco. It's a triumph. What thoroughness! What realism! Knew when to stop, too – didn't cut the pages." (3)*

As the reference to Belasco, the most famous stage producer on Broadway, suggests, Gatsby treats his library like a theatre set. It is there to impress not to inform the mind, and it reminds the reader how shallow the world of *The Great Gatsby* is, a world where no one reads – except Tom Buchanan who, typically, is reading a fascist tract – and where personality is self-created, "merely a series of gestures".

SIX KEY QUOTES

“These reveries provided an outlet for his imagination; they were a satisfactory hint of the unreality of reality, a promise that the rock of the world was founded securely on a fairy's wing.” (6)

“The truth was that Jay Gatsby of West Egg, Long Island, sprang from his platonic conception of himself.” (6)

“If personality is an unbroken series of successful gestures, then there was something gorgeous about him.” (1)

“He must have looked up at an unfamiliar sky through frightening leaves and shivered as he found what a grotesque thing a rose is and how raw the sunlight was upon the scarcely created grass. A new world, material without being real, where poor ghosts, breathing dreams like air, drifted fortuitously about.” (8)

“For a transitory enchanted moment man must have held his breath in the presence of this continent, compelled into an aesthetic contemplation he neither understood or desired, face to face for the last time in history with something commensurate to his capacity for wonder.” (9)

“Gatsby believed in the green light, the orgastic future that year by year recedes before us. It eluded us then, but that's no matter – tomorrow we will run faster, stretch out our arms further... And one fine morning –

So we beat on, boats against the current, born back ceaselessly into the past.” (9)

The Great Gatsby doesn't just fail to explore the inner lives of its characters; it suggests that they don't really have them. More than that, it suggests they can't have them. In this society of stylish drifters, a society with no real values, that has lost its morals and revolves around parties, it is not possible, the novel implies, to have anything which might plausibly be called "an inner life".

Is Gatsby's dream always doomed?

Daisy (née "Fay" – or "fairy"), the girl whom Gatsby dreams about, is almost as insubstantial as he is. She comes over to the reader as little more than a laugh and an aura. As Kathleen Parkinson puts it, she seems like "a charming wraith, a being who exists only as a fragile veneer, a shining radiance of Gatsby's construction" rather than as a woman with a personality of her own. She is allowed to exist only in the images others have of her. Thus we hear of her past from others, never directly from her: we are told of it by Jordan and later by Nick, and then he is only passing on what he has been told by Gatsby. The effect of this is to add to her nebulousness and make it seem as if she exists only as the object of a dream.

This is underlined by the stress put on her voice. We hear Daisy while never really seeing her.

In Chapter One Nick talks of the power of her voice: it is "thrilling", he says; it "compelled" him. We hear of her voice "glowing and singing" and of her "breathless, thrilling words". There is an echo, as Parkinson says, of "the powerful enchantment of the siren on the rocks who drew passing sailors to their doom". And more than that:

> *It was the kind of voice that the ear follows up and down, as if each speech is an arrangement of notes that will never be played again. Her face was sad and lovely, with bright things in it, bright eyes and a bright passionate mouth, but there was an excitement in her voice that men who had cared for her found difficult to forget; a singing compulsion, a whispered "Listen", a promise that she had done gay, exciting things just a while since and that there were gay, exciting things hovering in the next hour. (1)*

In the same chapter Daisy herself remarks:

> *"I looked outdoors for a minute... There's a bird on the lawn that I think must be a nightingale come over on the Cunard or White Star Line. He's singing away..."*

The allusion is to Keats's "Ode to a Nightingale",

in which the bird's song, in an ecstatic moment, seems to transcend pain and conduct the poet into the "Land of Faerie".

Virginal white is Daisy's colour. She passed her "white girlhood" with Jordan. She dressed in white and even her sporty little roadster was white. When Nick sees her on the sofa in Chapter One, she is also dressed in white; when she kisses Gatsby, her "white face came up to his own"; and Nick at one point imagines her "high in a white palace" (7).

She is typically associated with flowers – her name, of course, being that of a white flower. On

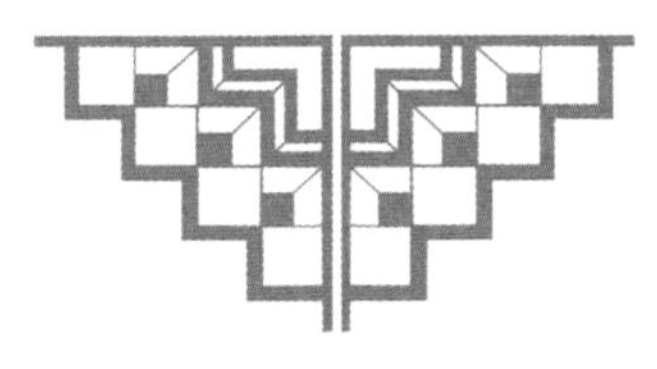

WHAT, EXACTLY, IS GATSBY'S "RACKET"?

Is Gatsby a mobster? The novel does not give us a clear answer, but throws out provocative hints. What is certain is that he is in cahoots with Meyer Wolfshiem. It may even have been Gatsby who rubbed out the man whose molars the gangster has fashioned into cufflinks. "I made him", says Wolfshiem to Nick. Made him what?

Gatsby is, he vaguely informs Nick, in the "drug business" – by which he means drugstores, or chemist shops. During Prohibition, these retailers could sell grain alcohol ("methylated spirits") for medicinal purposes (to dress wounds, principally). More significantly, they could order large amounts of the stuff and sell it on, under the counter, to bootleggers likely to concoct their rotgut brews.

arriving at the Buchanans' house, Nick moves through what he hyperbolically describes as "a half acre of deep pungent roses" before arriving at the "rosy-coloured space" of the drawing room (1); later the crimson room "bloomed with light"; she herself "blossomed" for Gatsby "like a flower" and her "artificial world", we are told, "was redolent of orchids".

These images catch her fragility, while the way she is associated with precious metals hints at her hardness and the superficiality of her charms. The house she shares with Tom glows "with reflected gold"; Nick fantasises about her, in an appropriately fairytale way, living high in her white palace – "the king's daughter, the golden girl" (7). When we first see her and Jordan, at the beginning of the narrative, they are stretched out on a couch "like silver idols". Later, when describing Gatsby's passion for her, Nick sees her "gleaming like silver". Never for a moment does it really seem likely that she will end up with Gatsby.

His dream is always an impossible one. When he invents himself, aged 17, "fantastic conceits" haunt him and "a universe of ineffable gaudiness spun itself out in his brain". His reveries, says Nick, "provided an outlet for his imagination; they were a satisfactory hint of the unreality of reality, a promise that the rock of the world was founded securely on a fairy's wing".

This passage, underlining the extravagance

of Gatsby's fantasies, comes – significantly – just after his meeting with Daisy in the middle of the novel. It is the moment when Gatsby comes closest to being happy. When he says goodbye and leaves them together, Nick sees a bewildered look pass over Gatsby's face, as if a "faint doubt" had struck him about the quality of his present happiness:

> *There must have been moments even that afternoon when Daisy tumbled short of his dreams – not through her own fault, but through the colossal vitality of his illusion.* (5)

When Daisy and Gatsby meet for a second time, at another of his parties, Gatsby is restless and depressed when she finally leaves. Nick guesses that what he wants is for Daisy to go to Tom and pledge that she's never loved him and then, having "obliterated four years with that sentence", go back to Louisville with him, Gatsby, and be married from her family house, "as if it were five years ago".

But she doesn't understand this, Gatsby explains to Nick as they walk up and down "a desolate path of fruit rinds and discarded favours and crushed flowers". The image conveys the hopelessness of Gatsby's dream: Daisy is lost to him and nothing will ever bring her back. His hopes have never been based on anything anyway, certainly not on anything real, as the next passage suggests, when Gatsby tells Nick what actually happened five years ago and the lovers first kissed:

> *He knew that when he kissed the girl, and forever wed his unutterable visions to her perishable breath, his mind would never romp again with the mind of God. (6)*

This can be taken as one of Nick's typically overblown conceits, but it is a poignant reminder of one of the novel's themes: that nothing can ever live up to our conception of it and that after his kiss the best is over for Gatsby. Catherine

GATSBY BELIEVED IN THE GREEN LIGHT

The green light has both a symbolic and literal meaning. But it is seldom asked what a green light is actually *doing* at the end of Tom Buchanan's dock. The nautical explanation is given by "madmariner" on his salt-encrusted website. The Buchanans' green light is a warning to vessels negotiating the tricky Manhasset Bay which may be veering dangerously close to the East Egg shore:

> The color-coding of lights is consistent. *Green lights* are placed atop green buoys as well as green and red buoys with horizontal bands in which green is the topmost color. If you see one of these, you know it is marking the left-hand side of the channel as you return from sea.

Belsey argues that desire is by its very nature unfulfillable: it is "predicated on lack, and even its apparent fulfilment is also a moment of loss". Whether or not we accept this – real desire, it might be argued, is "predicated" upon the joy of sharing mutual happiness, and its fulfilment leads to further such joys – the novel certainly suggests that Gatsby's passion is unreal and can never be satisfied.

In his magisterial *Passion and Society*, a brilliant discussion of passion in western life and literature, first published in France in 1939, Denis de Rougemont shows that grand passion depends for its very existence on obstacles and that its only, or kindest, resolution is death. He traces western ideas of passion to the 12th-century myth of Tristan and Iseult, a story in which the two lovers (whose love is triggered by a potion they take unwittingly) go out of their way to feed their love by finding obstacles to it: Tristan is always going away from Iseult when he doesn't need to, and at one point even puts his sword between them to keep them apart as they lie in a forest. What they love, says de Rougemont, is love itself and being in love – and they deliberately create "hindrances" to sustain their passion. "What they need is not one another's presence but one another's absence... The more Tristan loves, the more he wants to be parted from the beloved." We are in no doubt that if the obstacles were to vanish, and he were to marry her, his desire would vanish in an instant. "She is the woman-from-whom-one-is-parted."

The tremendous success of the Tristan romance, says de Rougemont, suggests that "we have a secret preference for what is unhappy" in our literature. We take a subversive delight in stories about "impossible love"; it occurs, in one form or another, again and again in western novels, from Edgar Allan Poe to Baudelaire, from Flaubert to André Gide, from *Anna Karenina* to the great Victorian novels, especially *Tess of the d'Urbervilles* and *Jude the Obscure.*

It occurs in *The Great Gatsby*, too: Daisy may be an unworthy object of grand passion – rich white trash with "old money" in her voice – but Gatsby believes totally in his love while at the same time being aware, deep down, that it cannot live up to its promise.

Obsessed as he is, he can never come to terms with Daisy's relationship with Tom. Late in the novel, when he tells Nick about her marriage, he insists she can never have loved Tom and describes how he had gone back to Louisville to try to recapture the moment they were together there. "He stretched out his hand desperately as if to snatch only a wisp of air, to save a fragment of the spot that she had made lovely for him." (8)

The symbol of Gatsby's dream is the green light on the dock below Daisy's mansion which he stares at night after night (see p.50). It provides a focus for his yearning and its power is related to its inaccessibility, to the fact that it is separated from Gatsby by a stretch of water. When Daisy is with him at his house and they look at the light together, it loses its power:

> *...the colossal significance of that light had now vanished forever. Compared to the great distance that had separated him from Daisy it had seemed as close as a star to the moon. Now it was again a green light on a dock. His count of enchanted objects had diminished by one. (5)*

In reality, Daisy can never match up to what the green light represents. In the same way, when Gatsby's father turns up for his funeral at the end of the book, he has in his pocket a tattered, dirty photograph of his son's house which he shows Nick with pride. Nick comments that he had handed it round so often that it was "more real to him" than the house itself.

Even after Myrtle Wilson has been run over and killed, Gatsby clings to his dream of Daisy. His only thought is his all-consuming passion. "I don't think she ever loved [Tom]," he says, and "Of course she might have loved him just for a minute, when they were first married – and loved me more even then, do you see?" (8) Gatsby's whole being, his very existence, have come to depend on his belief in his dream and nothing can be allowed to shatter it. And it is at this point, appropriately, as he and Gatsby sit talking through the night until dawn when "ghostly birds began to sing among the blue leaves", that Nick fills in the crucial final details of Gatsby's romance, and his despair at the loss of Daisy in 1919:

> *...he knew he lad lost that part of it, the freshest and the best, forever... (8)*

MEYER WOLFSHIEM/ ARNOLD ROTHSTEIN

Who is Wolfshiem, Nick asks Jay. "He's a gambler", Jay replies, "he's the man who fixed the World Series back in 1919." No reader of 1925 would need more information than that one remark. Meyer Wolfshiem is (historically) Arnold Rothstein (1882–1928).

Nicknamed "the Brain", "Mr Big" and "the Fixer" Rothstein was the smartest and slipperiest of the "Jewish gangsters" who ruled the New York underworld before the Italians took over in the late 1920s. Rothstein lives on in *The Great Gatsby* (and more romantically as "Nathan Detroit", in Damon Runyon's *Guys and Dolls*). His main money came from gambling and his most notorious crime was to "fix" the 1919 World Series baseball result by bribing members of the White Sox (Chicago) team to throw a match against the Cincinnati Reds. Rothstein was shot and killed in 1928, three years after his immortalisation as Meyer Wolfshiem. The murderer was never identified.

Fitzgerald was always frank about the sources for his characters. He wrote to

How much does money matter in the novel?

The corrupting influence of money is a theme which runs through all of Scott Fitzgerald's work. It was an *idée fixe* which he reiterated many times in different ways, and a core belief in *The Great Gatsby*.

In the weeks immediately following the novel's

Maxwell Perkins: "Jordan Baker of course was a great idea (perhaps you know it's Edith Cummings)." For Tom Buchanan, Fitzgerald drew on the husband of his first love, Ginevra, who came from an extremely wealthy Chicago banking family. Though Fitzgerald finally married Zelda, he described the wound inflicted by Ginevra as "the skin wound on a haemophile": "The whole idea of Gatsby is the unfairness of a poor young man not being able to marry a girl with money. This theme comes up again and again because I lived it."

"Owl Eyes" was based on Fitzgerald's close friend, Ring Lardner. The author had spent time with him and his family in their house on Great Neck – the setting for *The Great Gatsby*. A sportswriter in his early days, Lardner had travelled as team reporter with the Chicago White Sox and was nicknamed by the players "Owl Eyes". In the mid-1920s Lardner was best known as a humourist and short story writer. An alcoholic, he is depicted in his broken-down later years as Abe North in *Tender is the Night*. Lardner read *The Great Gatsby* in manuscript and made various corrections (about the layout of Penn Central Station, for example). He advised Fitzgerald against the early title *Trimalchio*. He evidently did not object to the depiction of himself in the novel.

publication, Fitzgerald worked on a long short story called "The Rich Boy", in which one of the characters famously says:

> *Let me tell you about the very rich. They are different from you and me. They possess and enjoy early, and it does something to them, makes them soft where we are hard, and cynical where we are trustful, in a way that, unless you were born rich, it is very difficult to understand. They think, deep in their hearts, that they are*

NEWLY RICH

The Fitzgeralds moved into a house in Great Neck ("West Egg") in October 1922, a month after the great (fictional) calamity at the conclusion of *The Great Gatsby*.

They rented their house for $300 a month (Nick pays $80 for his) and "bought a swank, although second-hand, Rolls coupé" – not quite equivalent to Jay's charabanc-sized Rolls, but classy. In Great Neck, as Fitzgerald said, they lived the life of the "newly rich":

> That is to say, five years ago we had no money at all, and what we now do away with would have seemed like inestimable riches to us then. I have at times suspected that we are the only newly rich people in America.

Their late West Egg neighbour, Jay Gatsby, could have said the same. It was at Great Neck that Fitzgerald first met his other mournful (and witty) neighbour, Ring Lardner – Owl Eyes in the novel.

opposite: The Fitzgeralds in 1927, two years after The Great Gatsby *was published*

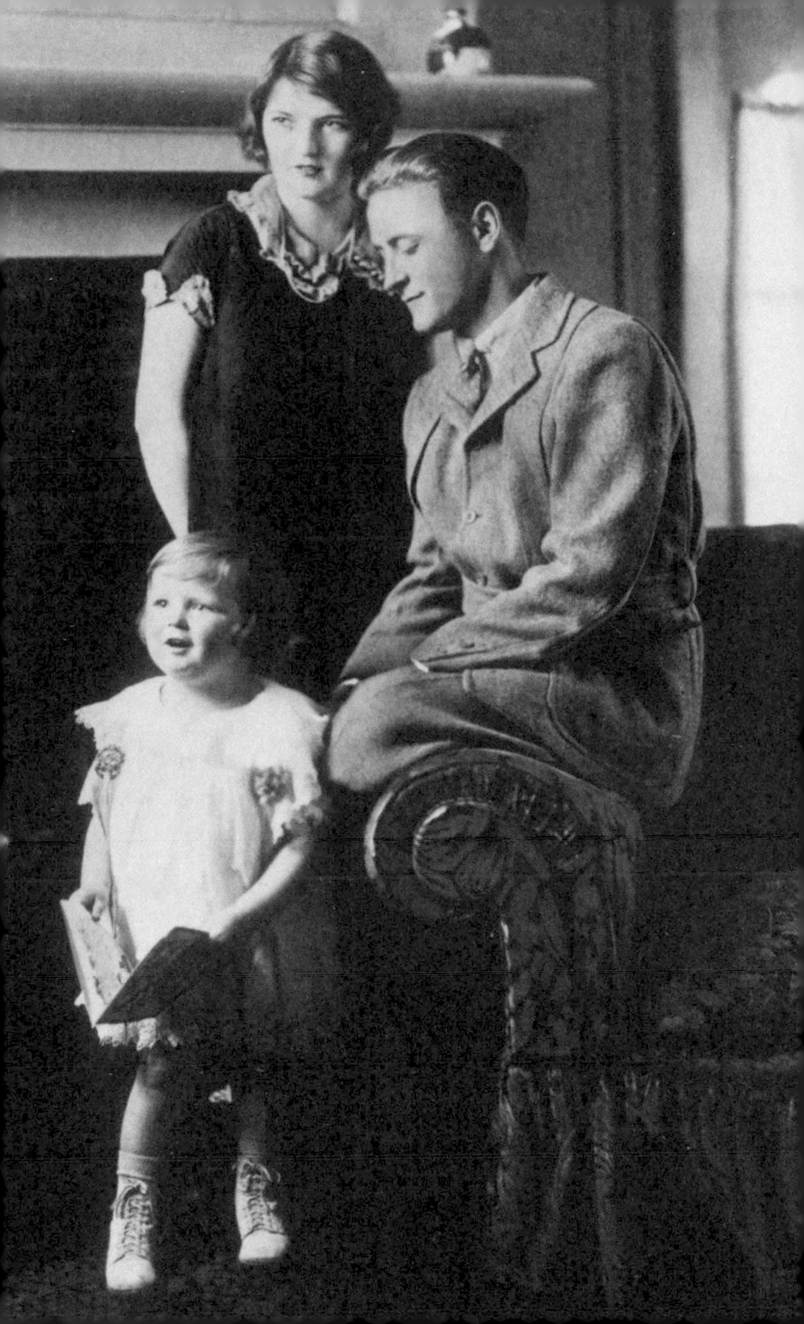

better than we are because we had to discover the compensations and refuges of life for ourselves. Even when they enter deep into our world or sink below us, they still think that they are better than we are. They are different.

It is not enough to retort, as Ernest Hemingway flippantly did, "Yes they have more money". The question of what exactly the "difference" is between rich and un-rich was, for Fitzgerald, a serious question, and one which never ceased to trouble him. Three years before his death he wrote, in an extravagance of self-pity:

That was always my experience – a poor boy in a rich

FITZGERALD AND MONEY

Fitzgerald's concern with what it is to be poor in *The Great Gatsby* needs to be kept in perspective. Like T.S. Eliot (and, among others, Longfellow and Oliver Wendell Holmes), he was a Brahmin, the name given to a group of New England writers associated with Harvard and Cambridge, Massachusetts, who were clever, steeped in foreign culture and – compared to most people, at least – wealthy. Fitzgerald never knew real poverty and can't summon much more sense of what it is to be a George Wilson than T.S. Eliot can of what it is to be a working-class Londoner in the "Cockney" section of *The Waste Land*. As a writer,

> town; a poor boy in a rich boy's school; a poor boy in a rich man's club at Princeton... I have never been able to forgive the rich for being rich and it has coloured my entire life and works. [*see below*]

So when Gatsby says, in explaining to Nick what makes Daisy magical, that "her voice is full of money", he evokes, above all, her *unapproachability* by anyone who doesn't have "money in their voice". What she has, as Nick elsewhere puts it, is "non-olfactory money" – money that doesn't smell of its origins. In Daisy's world, and in Tom's, *making* money, as Gatsby has, is very different to having been *made by* money over generations, as they have.

Theodore Dreiser, the author of *The American Tragedy*, which appeared in 1925, is no match for Fitzgerald. But he knew about the lives and dreams of poor as well as rich Americans, and his book reflects the misery of growing up in poverty better than anything Fitzgerald ever wrote.

Fitzgerald may have sensed this, in a characteristically unsteady way, when he wrote a misjudged forward to the 1934 Modern Library Edition of *The Great Gatsby* (so misjudged, in fact, that he realised it himself, and tried to recall and rewrite it, but it was too late):"But my God! It was my material and it was all I had to deal with." It was indeed all he had, and, to be harsh, it was the material of an alcoholic Princeton playboy. It is unlikely that Fitzgerald's near-contemporary, William Faulkner, the author of *The Sound and the Fury* and a man with his roots in America's Deep South, would have made this kind of excuse. He had so much more "material".

It's a crucial difference. When Lieutenant Gatsby meets Daisy in 1917, she inhabits a world quite unlike his, one that he can see, as through a pane of glass, but, he feels, never enter. He has never "been in such a beautiful house before"; were he not wearing a uniform, which disguises his poverty, he would never have set foot in it. He becomes aware of how fresh her clothes are and of how wealth "imprisons and preserves" youth and thus extends it. Daisy seems to him to be "gleaming like silver, safe and proud above the hot struggles of the poor".

Gatsby belongs with the hot struggles of the poor and always will, despite his Rolls Royce and his suits and shirts, sent across the Atlantic from his Jermyn Street tailor. When he takes her virginity, it is chronicled in a way which stresses the difference between him and Daisy: "eventually he took Daisy one still October night, took her because he had no real right to touch her hand". The verb "take" reminds us of Quasimodo, abducting Esmeralda (because he will never be able to kiss her lips), in *The Hunchback of Notre Dame.*

Is there a hint of rape in the phrase, or of something close to it? Possibly, but while it is no more than a hint, just as it is only hinted that Gatsby may have "killed a man", the blunt word "took" suggests that the impulse – the demand for physical fulfilment – was all on his side and that there was a certain reticence, even disgust, on hers. It is a perception which makes sense of the tragic denouement when she, fatally, declines to commit to the man who will (literally) give his life for her.

The phrase suggests, on Gatsby's side, the idea of *possession*. He "took" Daisy, as one might steal something which belongs to someone else. It is as if this girl, "gleaming like silver", is like the precious metals with which she is often compared; she is not quite human to Gatsby; she is an aura, something unattainable, and there is something warped about his romanticism and something strange about a dream based on a girl who comes to him not out of mutual desire or love but who has to be taken against her will. She represents his passport to a different world, his escape from the struggling poor. But she will always be beyond his grasp.

Only near the end of the novel do we learn just how poor Gatsby once was. His father, when he comes for the funeral, shows Nick a list of resolutions his son made as a child in the fly-leaf of his copy of *Hopalong Cassidy*: they include "Bath every other day" and "Save $5.00 [crossed out] $3 a week". Later, after the war, Gatsby was so hard up, according to Meyer Wolfshiem, that he had to keep on wearing his uniform because he couldn't afford "regular clothes". When the two men first met, Gatsby hadn't eaten for two days. "'Come on have some lunch with me,' I said. He ate more than four dollars' worth of food in half an hour."

In the end, of course, Daisy reverts to type. She may, for one brief moment before her wedding, have had second thoughts about chucking Gatsby for Tom and she even throws the $350,000 white pearl necklace Tom gives her in the wastepaper basket. But, counseled by Jordan, she soon retrieves it and marries the rich man. She is not prepared to slum it and while Gatsby struggles with the poor, she and her husband go off to Hawaii, California and Europe, living the life of wealthy drifters.

But her money doesn't make her happy. Fitzgerald shows her to be listless, spoilt and even, it is hinted, frigid. She is utterly self-absorbed and self-interested. She has no sense of purpose in life whatsoever (in ironic juxtaposition to Gatsby himself, whose love for her is what gives his life purpose). She and Jordan engage in talk that has "a bantering inconsequence" and "that was as cool as their white dresses and their impersonal eyes in the absence of all desire". As Susan Parr has noted, on several occasions her laments of boredom echo the voices in the "A Game of Chess" section of *The Waste Land*: "What'll we do with ourselves this afternoon... and the day after that, and the next thirty years?"

How does Gatsby compare with Tom?

In Chapter Eight, when Gatsby leaves Nick's house after having had breakfast with him, Nick calls out to him:

> *"They're a rotten crowd... You're worth the whole damn bunch put together."*

It is a crucial moment in the novel. Nick's judgement has been swinging to and fro about Gatsby – in Chapter Seven he is wanting "to get up and slap

GREAT?

In the published text there is, after the title, no reference to Gatsby being "great". In an early manuscript version of the novel, however, Fitzgerald had Gatsby boast to Nick, "There goes the great Jay Gatsby. That's what people are going to say – wait and see." Fitzgerald excised this single reference. Why? Because for Gatsby himself to proclaim his own "greatness" (like some precursor of Muhammad Ali) would look like vanity; and Gatsby is – if anything – a humble man. It is for others (and readers) to make the judgement, or not. Fitzgerald's instincts were right in excising this boast. It is one of innumerable examples of his attention to detail in the writing and revision of his manuscript.

TEN FACTS ABOUT *THE GREAT GATSBY*

1.

At barely 50,000 words, *The Great Gatsby* is the shortest of the so-called "Great American Novels", less than a third as long as *Moby Dick*.

2.

Fitzgerald had trouble publishing *The Great Gatsby* in England – his English publisher, William Collins, remarked that "to publish *The Great Gatsby* would be to reduce the number of his readers rather than to increase them". Eventually, it was published by Chatto & Windus, but only in a print run of 3,000 copies.

3.

Of the 450 "time" words in the novel, the critic Matthew Bruccoli has calculated it is the word "time" itself which crops up the most – no less than 87 times, the second most frequent word in the book (beaten into second place by "house", which occurs 95 times). The others are, in descending order: moment/s (73); day/s (70); minute/s (49); hour/s (47); o'clock (26); year (19); past (18); month/s (15); week/s (15); twilight (9); clock (9); watch (as in wristwatch) (5); future (5); time-table (3).

4.

In the 21st century *The Great Gatsby* is among the two or three most studied works of fiction in British and American schools and universities. It sells, it is estimated, some 500,000 copies every year, outselling all other works of Fitzgerald's combined by a margin of four to one.

5.

The Great Gatsby's narrative covers three summer months in 1922. It was an *annus mirabilis* for literature: the year in which James Joyce's *Ulysses,* T. S. Eliot's *The Waste Land,* and Virginia Woolf's *Jacob's Room* were published, as well as F. Scott Fitzgerald's *Tales of the Jazz Age*.

6.

The original cover of *The Great Gatsby* is a famous one. It features a disembodied woman's face, with reclining nude women for pupils, hovering above the bright lights of an amusement park. Completed by a little known artist named Francis Cugat before the novel was finished, a delighted Fitzgerald told his publisher that he had "written it into" the novel, giving rise to the idea that the eyes inspired those of Dr T.J. Eckleburg, "blue and gigantic – their retinas are one yard high", with his "non-existent nose", or even the description of Daisy as the "girl whose disembodied face floated along the dark cornices and blinding signs".

7.

Three major films have been made of *The Great Gatsby*. A silent movie, now lost, was made in 1926; a 1949 Paramount film, and the 1974 film starring Robert Redford and Mia Farrow, with a script by Francis Ford Coppola. Recently, the novel has been turned into a hip-hop movie, *G*, set in the Hamptons. And in 2008, the acclaimed though inconsistent director Baz Luhrmann announced that he had acquired the film rights to Fitzgerald's novel.

8.

Fitzgerald was popular amongst his peers. The Matthew J. and Arlyn Bruccoli Collection of F. Scott Fitzgerald's books includes books inscribed to him by Ernest Hemingway, James Joyce, Gertrude Stein, H.L. Mencken, John Dos Passos, Ring Lardner and Thomas Boyd.

9.

One of the novel's most famous fans is Holden Caulfield, the fictional protagonist of J.D. Salinger's *The Catcher in the Rye*. Speaking to his brother, Holden said: "I still don't see how he could like a phony book like [Hemingway's *A Farewell to Arms*] and still like that one by Ring Lardner or that other one he's so crazy about, *The Great Gatsby*...I was crazy about *The Great Gatsby*. Old Gatsby. Old Sport. That killed me."

10.

Fitzgerald was a notoriously poor speller. The novel's famous and mysterious "coda" features the esoteric word "orgastic". Fitzgerald's posthumous editor, Edmund Wilson, assumed this was yet another example of the writer's careless spelling, and corrected it to "orgiastic", and several posthumous editions carried this emendation. But Wilson was unaware that Fitzgerald had already thrashed out the orgiastic/orgastic issue with Maxwell Perkins, his editor. Perkins had also queried the apparent misspelling. Fitzgerald replied, defiantly: "'Orgastic' is the adjective from 'orgasm' and it expresses exactly the intended ecstasy."

him on the back" after he silences Tom in an argument; a few pages later, when they meet after the accident, he decides he thoroughly dislikes him. Now he finally sides with a non-plussed Gatsby, telling him he is worth more than the "old money" types like Tom who patronise and despise him.

Whether or not he has actually killed a man – a rumour repeated several times – Gatsby has certainly let a friend of Tom's take the rap for an illegal deal, he is almost certainly a boot-legger and is undoubtedly an illegal bond trader. Towards the end of the novel the staff at his house are sacked and replaced by goons from the Mob. But he is generous and brave, behaves with an authentic nervousness bordering on panic when about to meet Daisy, and above all he believes in something – his "incorruptible dream", as Nick calls it.

Tom, on the other hand, is a gangster in all but name: he is sadistic, violent, racist and, like those around him, a cheat. (Jordan cheats at golf, Myrtle cheats on her husband, Daisy conceals the fact that she was driving the "death car".) Although he floats on a sea of "old" Chicago money, washed clean by generations of "enormous" family banking wealth, Tom is portrayed as a worthless drifter and bully, who not only wasn't a war hero like Gatsby, but who didn't even go to war in 1917. Thus it was he was able to steal another man's promised bride – Daisy Fay.

And having married her, Tom is then, almost

immediately, unfaithful, his first infidelity occurring immediately after their honeymoon, only days after he has lain on a beach with his head on Daisy's lap. When the narrative opens, he is cuckolding simple George Wilson, of whom he says, contemptuously: "He's so dumb he doesn't know he's alive." Eventually he will drive dumb Wilson to his death. He does so without remorse.

It's notable that in the two cases of his infidelity that we hear about – with the Californian chambermaid and with Myrtle – Tom chooses women of much lower social standing than himself and his wife. In a twisted way, his behaviour emerges as a kind of fidelity, enabling him to say in the climactic Plaza Hotel scene: "Once in a while I go off on a spree and make a fool of myself, but I always come back, and in my heart I love her [Daisy] all the time" (7). Poor people – chambermaids and garage-owners' wives – don't count. He doesn't love them, he uses them for his body's needs and, once used, discards them.

What Tom conveniently blurs in his use of the word "spree" is that he has lied cruelly to Myrtle. According to her sister Catherine (Myrtle's "cover story" when she comes to New York), Myrtle and her husband have been "living over that garage for eleven years. And Tom's the first sweetie she's ever had" (2). Tom, Catherine adds, has told her: "it's really his wife that's keeping them apart. She's a Catholic, and they don't believe in divorce." Daisy isn't a Catholic. Myrtle nonetheless fondly believes Tom will elope with her (and the dog he has bought her). That vain hope is why she dashes into the road, and to her death, under the wheels of a woman whose name she is forbidden from uttering.

The Great Gatsby is full of casual violence. At the end of the party described in Chapter Three, for example, a woman has a fight with a man who "says he's her husband"; Nick comments that most of the remaining women were also "having fights with men said to be their husbands". In the next scene, when Nick has lunch with Gatsby and Wolfshiem in New York, the talk is of a gangster who is "shot four times in his full belly" (and of his killers going to the electric chair). Gatsby is thought to have killed a man himself. Tom casually breaks his mistress's nose; one of Gatsby's party guests has his hand run over (all the parties around which the novel revolves end badly in one way or another); and the story ends with a hit-and-run death, a murder and a suicide. Throughout, we are reminded that reality is very different to our dreams – and that dreams bear only the most tenuous connection to the real world. But while Nick suggests that even Gatsby himself has moments when he realises his dream is hopeless, he never loses faith in it. It has become his "mode of combat", as Conrad says of Lord Jim when Jim tries to hold on to

his own shattered dream.*

Tom, on the other hand, is no more than a brute and while Gatsby may have made his money illegally, the novel suggests Tom is the more morally worthless of the two. He has nothing whatever to recommend him. Gatsby, at least, believes in something and is prepared to die for it. We are given no reason to doubt Nick's final judgement that Gatsby is worth "the whole damn bunch put together".

What does *The Great Gatsby* tell us about the American Dream?

The Great Gatsby was written by Fitzgerald in a mood of deep pessimism. He would argue later that he had been in the midst of reading Oswald Spengler's book, *The Decline of the West*, while writing the novel, and that he was strongly affected by the German philosopher's grim view of the

* Marlow is considering what to make of Jim's sudden shifts, the restless way he gives up jobs and suddenly moves on: is he running away from himself and his dreams – or trying to face reality? "What I could never make up my mind about was whether his line of conduct amounted to shirking his ghost or to facing him out.

"I strained my mental eyesight only to discover that, as with the complexion of all our actions, the shade of difference was so delicate that it was impossible to say. It might have been flight and it might have been a mode of combat."

likely doom of western civilization and democracy.

The novel has an elegiac tone, and it is an elegy not merely for the empty life, the unappreciated generosity (towards his party guests as well as Daisy), wretched death and unattended funeral of its hero, but also for the American Dream itself. If there was anything spiritual and uplifting in this dream, the book implies, it was lost, almost immediately, overpowered by greed and a lust for money and possessions. What might have been a wonderland has been turned into a wasteland, decadent, rotten to the core, as over the top and doomed as Gatsby. The green light he stares at night after night is like the white light in Matthew Arnold's "Dover Beach", which the hero looks at from across the Channel until it finally goes out, suggesting the light of republicanism in France has also been extinguished.

Fitzgerald wasn't the first novelist to show the seamier side of the American Dream. Fifty years before *The Great Gatsby*, Mark Twain published *The Gilded Age: A Tale of Today*, a book co-written with his neighbour, Charles Dudley Warner, which satirised post-Civil War America. Taking their title from Shakespeare's *King John* – "To gild refined gold, to paint the lily... is wasteful and ridiculous excess" – Twain and Warner wrote about the corruption, conspicuous consumption and greed which lay beneath the glitter of late 19th-century America, a time, as they saw it, of robber barons, unscrupulous speculators, corporate buccaneers and vulgar display.

Twenty years earlier, in 1857, Herman Melville's prescient and devastating last novel, *The Confidence-Man*, had a similar theme. The novel has a *Canterbury Tales*-style group of steamboat passengers travelling down the Mississippi, all of them tricksters, like the "confidence man" of the title, or dupes. Just as *The Confidence-Man* anticipates Mark Twain in its pessimistic view of an America grown tawdry, so both pave the way for Fitzgerald's work in the 1920s.

After *The Great Gatsby* was published, Fitzgerald wrote to the author Marya Mannes:

> America's greatest promise is that something is going to happen, and after a while you get tired of waiting because nothing happens to people except that they grow old, and nothing happens to American art because America is the story of the moon that never rose.

When the moon does rise at the end of *The Great Gatsby* it prompts one of the book's most lyrical passages:

> *The inessential houses began to melt away until gradually I became aware of the old island here that flowered once for Dutch sailors' eyes – a fresh, green breast of the new world. Its vanished*

trees, the trees that had made way for Gatsby's house, had once pandered in whispers to the last and greatest of human dreams; for a transitory enchanted moment man must have held his breath in the presence of this continent, compelled into an aesthetic contemplation he neither understood or desired, face to face for the last time in history with something commensurate to his capacity for wonder. (9)

It is a powerful image. The "green breast of the new world" held out the promise of possible new life, an inexhaustible supply of the "milk of wonder". Instead the sailors who arrived on America's shores, all the sailors, came in one way or another to "rape it", as William Carlos Williams put it about the multiple spoliations of the American land.

As Tony Tanner says, Fitzgerald wanted to show America "desecrated, mutilated, violated" and he does so with a very different image of a breast, the shocking image of Myrtle's left breast "swinging loose like a flap" after the road accident, an image Fitzgerald insisted on retaining. "I want Myrtle Wilson's breast ripped off – it's exactly the thing, I think," he wrote to his editor in December 1924.

The interest of the settlers who "raped" the land was narrow and self-interested – the acquisition of wealth, no matter what it took. And while Nick and Gatsby are acutely conscious of the difference between "new" and "old" money, the novel itself doesn't encourage us to make so much of the difference, or of the distinction between East Egg, the home of "new money" and therefore of Gatsby, and West Egg, across the Sound, where "old money" America lives. (The name Egg is ironic, of course, suggesting innocence and new life.) The two pieces of land, we are told "are not perfect ovals... but their physical resemblance must be a source of perpetual wonder to the gulls that fly overhead. To the wingless a more interesting phenomenon is their dissimilarity in every particular except shape and size." (1)

Nick himself later talks of the "sinister contrast" between the two Eggs but then this, as he himself acknowledges, is only his limited view – the

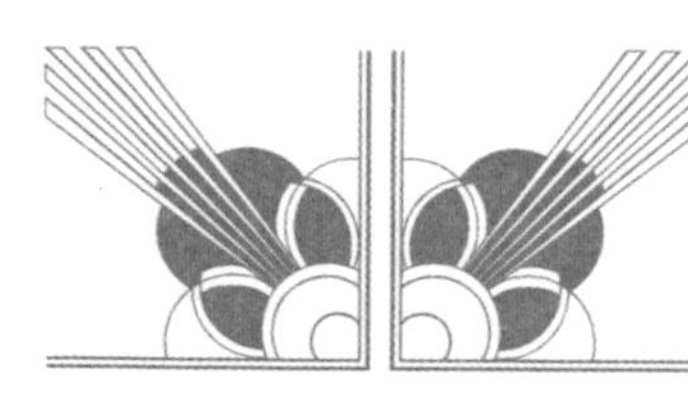

GATSBY'S HEROIC MILITARY CAREER (OR NOT)

On their first meeting, Gatsby tells Nick that his face is somehow familiar. "Weren't you in the Third Division during the war?" he asks. "Yes," Nick replies, "I was in the Ninth Machine-gun Battalion". "I was in the Seventh until June nineteen-eighteen," says Gatsby.

In Chapter Four, details of Gatsby's war heroism emerge in another conversation with Nick. He wanted to die "but I seemed to bear an enchanted life". In the Battle of the Argonne Forest, he recklessly took "the remains of my machine gun battalion" deep beyond the front lines. Three days

perspective of the "wingless". From a loftier point of view, the similarities are the source of "perpetual wonder": both are given over to crude materialism and the concept of "old money" means little.

And while Gatsby's dream is shown to be futile, Tom's world, a world of money and success in which the "dream" has been achieved, is shown as worse. It is fatuous, corrupt, even evil. His only concern is the survival of the rich – of his own small privileged world.

This is brought home to us when, in the middle of some very small talk during Nick's first visit to West Egg, Tom "breaks out" with the exclamation:

> *"Civilization's going to pieces ... I've gotten to be a terrible pessimist about things. Have you read*

---

later, his unit was surrounded by the dead, but emerged victorious, having fought off a German Divisional attack.

"I was promoted to be a Major," Gatsby recalls "and every Allied Government gave me a decoration – even Montenegro, little Montenegro down on the Adriatic Sea!" (4)

According to Ruth Prigozy, "Gatsby's participation in that battle [Argonne] makes his heroism unequivocal". But does it? The three Meuse-Argonne offensives, conducted by the US forces, took place from September to November 1918. Gatsby earlier told Nick he left the 16th Infantry in June of that year.

Is Gatsby's wartime heroism, like his big-game hunting and ruby collecting, just another tall story, designed to impress the rich folks? As with everything that Gatsby says, one has to be suspicious.

'The Rise of the Colored Empires' by this man Goddard?" (1)

Tom clearly refers to *The Rising Tide of Color: Against White World-Supremacy*, by Lothrop Stoddard, published in 1920. Tom's views derive from Stoddard and from his principal source, the "eugenicist" Madison Grant who, in his book *The Passing of the Great Race* (1916), divided the world's white peoples into Nordic, Alpine and Mediterranean. Nordics, argued Grant, were the superior strand. Tom, in his stress on "civilization" may also have dipped into another work of Stoddard's, published in 1922, *The Revolt Against Civilization: The Menace of the Under Man.* This is a quotation from it:

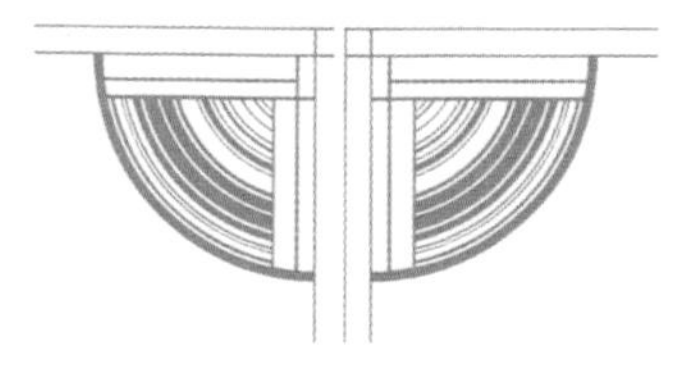

SCOTT FITZGERALD'S UNHEROIC MILITARY CAREER

On 26 October 1917, America having entered the war, Fitzgerald left Princeton and enlisted. He was transferred, while training, to Camp Taylor in Louisville, Kentucky, in February 1918. This is where, a few months earlier, Gatsby had been stationed, and where, in nearby Louisville, he fell in love with Daisy Fay. Fitzgerald completed his training at Montgomery, Alabama, where he fell in love with Zelda Sayre. He was commissioned as First Lieutenant in the 67th Infantry and posted in November 1918 to

> Here, then, was what had come to pass: instead of dying off at the base and growing at the top, civilized society was dying at the top and spreading out below. The result of this dual process was, of course, as disastrous as it was inevitable. Drained of its superiors, and saturated with dullards and degenerates, the stock could no longer support its civilization. And, the upper layers of the human foundation having withered away, the civilization either sank to a lower level or collapsed in utter ruin. The stock had regressed, "gone back", and the civilization went back too. Such are the workings of that fatal tendency to biological regression which has blighted past civilizations.

Long Island, to await assignment overseas. Hostilities ceased in that month. It was (with his failure to shine on the Princeton football field) one of the great disappointments of Fitzgerald's life not to have seen battle. As he told Michael Mok in 1936, "I *almost* went across. They actually marched us on to a transport and then marched us right off again. Influenza epidemic or something."

In *The Gun and the Pen: Hemingway, Fitzgerald, Faulkner and the Fiction of Mobilization*, Keith Gandal argues that the principal "American voices of the Great War" are defined not by the horror of war but the fact that they *failed* to have these experiences. These "quintessential" male novelists of the 1920s, he argues, were emasculated and alienated by their failure to qualify for full military service.

Tom Buchanan is, of course, as Nordic as his Scottish name. He believes in what he calls "Nordic" blood (his blood) and the need to protect it from the coloured and promiscuously breeding hordes who are destroying America's racial stock. He makes another telling remark on the theme later in the story when he says, disgustedly, that Gatsby's marrying Daisy would be as horrible as "intermarriage between black and white". It is not just the coloured races, but the lower classes, who are a danger to "civilization".

Fitzgerald clearly planted these precise references to racist tracts to underline Tom's oafishness. (The passage also anticipates the rise of fascism in the 1930s.) Even his house, a "red-and-white Georgian colonial mansion" with an "Italian garden" in fashionable East Egg originally belonged to an oil man, suggesting the sordid commerce which lies behind the opulent, exclusive, self-regarding surface. The "white palaces" of East Egg may glitter along the shoreline, but they are like white sepulchres, the book implies, hiding the moral shabbiness and indifference of their inhabitants. They may have more style than the houses in West Egg but they are no less false. The fact is that everyone is guilty: while Buchanan's house belonged to an oil man, Gatsby's house originally belonged to a brewer, equally significant in a novel where alcohol and cars (powered by oil) do so much damage. Tony Tanner writes:

> A brewer and an oil man: the money that could afford to erect these grandiose architectural masks, drawing on Europe and history for facades at once to cover and dignify the origins of their wealth, is derived from alcohol and oil, two of the basic raw materials that indeed serve to fuel much of American society, moving both the economy and the people in different and dangerous ways: think how much of the novel is taken up with drinking and driving – and drunken driving.

It is the Valley of Ashes, of course, not East or West Egg, which is the focal point of the novel and where the final fatal car crash occurs. A huge dumping ground for the detritus of an obsessively materialist society, it is a symbol, as Kathleen Parkinson puts it, of callousness and carelessness and "underlying despair". Nick sees the ash-heaps as a parody of life-enhancing growth; they are linked, inevitably, with sterility and death. The Valley is also, as it were, the metaphorical centre of the novel, generating, as it does what Nick calls the "foul dust" which he sees as floating "in the wake of [Gatsby's] dreams".*

A century earlier, Charles Dickens had conjured up a similar image, in the London dust-heaps that

* The Valley of Ashes actually existed, as Matthew Bruccoli has pointed out: known as the Corona dumps, the valley was 20 miles from New York, a piece of swamp that became a landfill for garbage, horse manure and ashes from coal-burning furnaces.

symbolise the darkness at the heart of Victorian capitalism in *Our Mutual Friend*. Gigantic heaps of urban excrement, for which the favoured euphemism was "ash", these dust heaps were a source of huge wealth for those who owned them. Nowhere in 19th-century England was lucre more filthy.

Dickens's novel was, in turn, one of the sources for *The Waste Land*. Universally acknowledged as the most important poem of the 20th century, this was published in 1922. Fitzgerald was steeped in *The Waste Land* and actually uses the title of the poem in his description of the Valley of Ashes: "The only building in sight was a small block of yellow brick sitting on the edge of the waste land..." (2) He took on the poem's bleak vision of postwar rottenness lying behind the shimmering facades of the 1920s – notably the poem's second paragraph from "What are the roots that clutch, what branches grow/Out of this stony rubbish" with its much quoted climax, "I will show you fear in a handful of dust".

It is significant that Fitzgerald uses Valley of Ashes – not "garbage", "rubbish", or "dust", each of which would fall more naturally from the tongue. Why? Because "ash" (like "valley" in the psalmic "valley of the shadow of death") has powerful liturgical undertones. In the Christian burial service, as earth is thrown on the coffin, the priest intones: "ashes to ashes, dust to dust". The religious overtones of the Valley of Ashes are enforced by the other dominant image in the novel, Dr Eckleburg's eyes. They stare out from a billboard, halfway between West Egg and East Egg, looking eternally, ominously and enigmatically, at – what? Everything and nothing:

> *Above the grey land and the spasms of bleak dust which drift endlessly over it, you perceive, after a moment, the eyes of Doctor T. J. Eckleburg. The eyes of Doctor T. J. Eckleburg are blue and gigantic – their retinas are one yard high.* * *They look out of no face, but, instead, from a pair of enormous yellow spectacles which pass over a non-existent nose. Evidently some wild wag of an oculist set them there to fatten his practice in the borough of Queens, and then sank down himself into eternal blindness, or forgot them and moved away. But his eyes, dimmed a little by many paintless days, under sun and rain, brood on over the solemn dumping ground. (2)*

Like Eliot's Tiresias in *The Waste Land*, Eckleburg is both blind and all-seeing. When the tragi-comic, cuckolded garage man Wilson goes crazy, he begins to confuse the great, fading billboard looming over his garage with the all-seeing eye of the Almighty,

* Fitzgerald does not, of course, mean "retina" but "iris". The author was sometimes careless about such details and this is one his hawk-eyed editor, Maxwell Perkins, did not spot.

suggesting not only that they are blind to human misery but also that business has become the new religion.

> *Wilson's glazed eyes turned out to the ashheaps, where small gray clouds took on fantastic shapes and scurried here and there in the faint dawn wind.*
>
> *"I spoke to her," he muttered, after a long silence. "I told her she might fool me but she couldn't fool God. I took her to the window" – with an effort he got up and walked to the rear window and leaned with his face pressed against it – "and I said, 'God knows what you've been doing, everything you've been doing. You may fool me, but you can't fool God!'"*
>
> *Standing behind him, Michaelis saw with a shock that he was looking at the eyes of Dr T. J. Eckleburg, which had just emerged... from the dissolving night.*
>
> *"God sees everything," repeated Wilson.*
>
> *"That's an advertisement," Michaelis assured him. (8)*

Fitzgerald's vision of America in *The Great Gatsby* is what Tony Tanner calls "entropic": he sees "the great agrarian continent turning itself into some sort of terminal rubbish heap or waste land, where, with ultimate perversity, the only thing that grows is death".

This process, as we have noted, is associated in

the novel with cars, of which the book is full (Jordan Baker's name is even made up of two types of car), and the implication is that they are not only killing people but the land itself. At the heart of the Valley of Ashes is Wilson's garage. On the one hand cars are seen as romantic, with Nick feeling excluded, for example, from the the life enjoyed by couples in "throbbing taxicabs" and much being made of Gatsby's own car. On the other, they are seen as destructive and violent.

There are five accidents in the narrative, and they become increasingly serious. Early on Jordan drives so close to a workman that the fender of her car flicks a button on his coat; Mrs Ulysses Swett's car runs over the right hand of a drunk on Gatsby's drive; Tom injures the chambermaid with whom he has an affair in Santa Barbara when he runs "into a wagon on the Ventura road one night" – the front wheel of his car, we hear, is "ripped off" in the crash. And in the final – fatal – accident, the word "ripped" comes in again, with Myrtle's mouth left "wide open and ripped a little at the corners..."

Myrtle, the poor working-class girl condemned to a life of drudgery and squalor in the Valley of Ashes, is destroyed by money and power. Kathleen Parkinson writes:

> The impersonal death machine violates Myrtle's female identity and ravages her: it is a symbolic rape. George Wilson deals in wrecks: "the only car visible

> was a dust-covered wreck of a Ford which crouched down in a dim corner." Both Tom and Gatsby are responsible for the social chasm dividing Wilson from them and relegating him to a dim corner of society; their wealth and their cars brutally destroy him.

How does Fitzgerald treat women in the novel?

If the novel is scathing in its treatment of men, it is even more damning in its attitude to women. In *The Resisting Reader*, the critic Judith Fetterley wrote crossly:

> Another American novel centred on hostility to women... Not dead Gatsby but surviving Daisy is the object of the novel's hostility and its scapegoat.

Fitzgerald, Fetterley argues, portrays America as female, writing of her green breast that "had once pandered to the last and greatest of all human dreams" (9), whereas the dreamers are male.

> Daisy's failure of Gatsby is symbolic of the failure of America to live up to the expectations in the imagination of the men who "discovered" it. America is female; to be American is male; and the quintessential American experience is betrayal by a woman.

opposite: Mia Farrow as Daisy Buchanan in the 1974 film

It is true that the women in *The Great Gatsby* are shown as incapable not just of idealism or artistic interests but of passion too. They are not even sexy: Nick, for example, asserts that Daisy is sexually exciting but nothing she says or does, and none of the descriptions of her, actually bring this quality out. Only lower-class Myrtle is shown to be sensual as she tells the story of her relationship with Tom.

The Great Gatsby, indeed, is rather a chaste novel. Fitzgerald never wrote well about sex, says the American critic Leslie Fiedler: "love", for him, was essentially yearning and frustration, and although he identified himself with the sexual revolution "which the 1920s thought of as their special subject," there is little consummated physical passion in his novels. "The adolescent's 'kiss' is the only climax his imagination can really encompass."*

When the novel failed, in its early days, to achieve commercial success, Fitzgerald himself acknowledged that women didn't like it – they did not like to be shown to be "emotionally passive", he said, which is precisely how they are shown in the novel.

* Hemingway, on the other hand, was "much addicted to describing the sex act". "There are, however," Fiedler adds, "no *women* in his books!" "In his earlier fictions, Hemingway's descriptions of the sexual encounter are intentionally brutal, in his later ones unintentionally comic; for in no case can he quite succeed in making his females human, and coitus performed with an animal, a thing, or a wet dream is either horrible or ridiculous."

> *On Sunday morning while church bells rang in the villages alongshore, the world and its mistress returned to Gatsby's house and twinkled hilariously on his lawn. (4)*

The men are "the world"; the women merely "its mistress". Their conversation shows a disregard not only for Gatsby but for anything serious such as the war. Shallow, devious and unscrupulous, their only concern, as Kathleen Parkinson stresses, is a desire for "a good time and for material possessions". Indeed any other interest than a preoccupation with their own needs is shown as beyond the women characters: trapped in a man's world, and dependent on men, they are decorative and to some extent sensuous but morally worthless. This is true not just of the old-money women, but of poor, under-privileged, lower-class Myrtle*.

Early on in the novel, when Tom takes Myrtle on a "spree" to New York, she buys a dog on impulse without any thought as to how she might look after it or where the dog might actually live. She simply buys it as she would a trinket, because she takes a fancy to it and Tom can afford it. Shallow and materialistic, she is also a terrible snob who says her husband wasn't "fit to lick my shoe": what really rankled was that he had to borrow

* Like Daisy, Myrtle is named after a plant, in her case a dark, hardy, non-flowering shrub. Nick Carraway is also named after a plant which produces caraway seeds.

"somebody's best suit" to get married in.

In the same way, she thinks of Tom in terms of his clothes: when she met him, she says, he "had on a dress-suit and patent leather shoes" and when they came out of the station together "his white shirt-front pressed against my arm".

The least passive of the women in *The Great Gatsby* is Jordan Baker, but significantly she, of all the women, behaves most like a man, and is described in very unfeminine terms. She is a "slender, small-breasted girl", we are told. She "wore all her dresses like sports clothes – there was a jauntiness about her movements as if she had first learned to walk upon golf courses on clean, crisp mornings" (3). A woman golfer in 1925 was something of an oddity, and there is a faint, but persistent, aura of mannishness about Jordan – even down to her androgynous name.

Does Nick's relationship with her imply that he is in fact a repressed homosexual, that it is Jordan's mannishness which attracts him and that his truly romantic feelings are taken up with Gatsby? It is left open. Certainly he is afraid of commitment and, the novel suggests, of sex as well. There is undoubtedly an element of misogyny in his attitude to Jordan, even if he is entirely right that she is "incurably dishonest", cannot bear being at a disadvantage and will do anything, even lie or cheat, to gain an advantage over others. He admires her shamelessness, or "honest dishonesty", however, noting that she had embarked on this course when she was young, maintaining her "cool, insolent smile" towards the world as a cover allowing her to satisfy "the demands of her hard, jaunty body" without being found out.

To some extent, of course, Nick's view of women reflects his patriarchal view of the world, with its implicit contempt for the notion of the "New Woman" and the values that he holds, but it is also true to Fitzgerald's vision of a society in which women were prized, and thus came to prize themselves, only for the way they appeared and their ability to win and hold men.

If Jordan is incurably dishonest, Daisy is in every important way morally reprehensible. To Gatsby, she is and remains a dream figure, as distant as the green light burning at the end of her dock which mesmerises him. It is a symbol of the unattainable. Yet when he is with her, looking at the light, he scarcely seems conscious that the actual Daisy is beside him and they never have much to say to one another. The light is more real to him than Daisy, bearing out de Rougemont's view of the self-centred, narcissistic nature of passion and Freud's dictum that we love our desires more than the desired. Daisy is imprisoned, for him, in the view he had of her five years earlier and nothing can be allowed to spoil that.

But the colossal vitality of the illusion is what,

ultimately, sustains Gatsby. In truth, Daisy is worthless, as we know more or less from the very first scene of the novel. She is disloyal and shallow and the decisions she makes at the end are self-interested and destructive and lead inevitably to Gatsby's death. She doesn't return to the scene of the accident or tell the police she was driving the car; she doesn't call Gatsby the day after the accident, or attend his funeral, or send a message or flowers, or make any attempt to contact him. It is, we realise, entirely appropriate that she should have married a brute like Tom and entirely understandable that she should stay with him. He is like a reflection of her, for she, too, is a monster of egotism.

When, after the fatal accident, Nick sneaks over to the Buchanan mansion, he sees Daisy and Tom through the kitchen window at the kitchen table. Tom

> *was talking intently across the table at her, and in his earnestness his hand had fallen upon and covered her own. Once in a while she looked up at him and nodded in agreement... There was an unmistakable air of natural intimacy about the picture, and anybody would have said that they were conspiring together. (7)*

We are never clear what they are conspiring about but it seems unlikely Daisy confesses to

Tom that she was driving the car which killed his mistress. It seems most likely that they are making arrangements to leave, immediately, and to keep away until the fuss dies down. Daisy, in other words, lies outright to save her skin, and her lie condemns Gatsby. Nick realizes she is worthless.

> *They were careless people, Tom and Daisy – they smashed up things and then retreated back into their money... and let other people clean up the mess they had made. (9)*

Gatsby dies not for a dream, but a false dream – a "dead dream", as Nick calls it. In a novel full of anti-climaxes, his death is handled in the same unmelodramatic, indirect way that Verloc's death is treated in Conrad's *The Secret Agent*. Verloc is stabbed by his wife, but all we are given is an impressionistic description of the shadow of an arm on a wall. Winnie Verloc commits suicide afterwards, like George Wilson, and the papers report the deaths as acts of madness. As he lies on his sun-mattress, floating listlessly in his pool, in the hour of his death, does Gatsby – at last – *know* that Daisy is unworthy of his devotion?

Probably not. Gatsby may know, deep down, that his dream is over and has always been hopeless, but he can't acknowledge this. Fitzgerald said romantics have "a desperate confidence that things won't last" and Gatsby is a romantic, even if his romanticism is warped, built on an unworthy object and an act of rough sex; indeed what gives the novel its power is the way it combines romanticism and despair. Fitzgerald, wrote the critic Arthur Mizener in 1963, is expressing both the feeling "that life is unendurable without a belief in the possibility of a meaningful existence" and the feeling "that the world conspires to make such a belief impossible".

What does the novel tell us about the nature of dreams?

Even though Nick realises that Daisy is essentially worthless, he remains in awe of the extraordinary power of Gatsby's dream, the "colossal vitality of his illusion":

> *It had gone beyond her, beyond everything. He had thrown himself into it with a creative passion, adding to it all the time, decking it out with every bright feather that drifted his way. No amount of freshness can challenge what a man will store up in his ghostly heart.* (5)

As for Nick, disillusioned by the grotesque scenes he has witnessed, he decides to go home again to the Midwest. He ends his relationship with Jordan in typically orderly style and decides he no longer wants complexity or to be a "well-rounded man"; instead he thinks "life is much more successfully looked at from a single window after all". Like Gatsby, though in his own tame, voyeuristic way, he opts to embrace his past even though, as Susan Parr puts it, "he knows that such a choice is itself based on illusions and romantic memories of childhood". So he ignores his knowledge of the Midwest as a place of "bored, sprawling, swollen towns beyond the Ohio, with their interminable inquisitions which spared only the children and the very old" in favour of his own vision of the place:

> *...not the wheat or the prairies or the lost Swede towns, but the thrilling returning trains of my youth, and the street lamps and sleigh bells in the frosty dark and the shadows of holly wreaths thrown by lighted windows on the snow. I am a part of that... (9)*

The Great Gatsby explores how compelling dreams can be. Without them, it implies, life is meaningless and we amount to nothing: Tom calls Gatsby "Mr Nobody from Nowhere" and Gatsby himself tells Nick early on: "I didn't want you to think I was just some nobody." Our sense of identity, the novel suggests, depends on and is shaped by our dreams: it is through them that we live.

But the book is also about the hollowness of dreams, and how by their very nature they can never be realised. When Gatsby's forebear, Trimalchio, is first seen in Petronius's story he is "busily engaged with a green ball. He never picked it up if it touched the ground." Gatsby's equivalent is the green light at the end of Daisy's dock. It provides a focus for his yearning and its power is related to its inaccessibility.

In reality, Daisy can never match up to the green light. Dreams are based on something which happens in the past, but the past can never be recaptured.

As Susan Parr says, for Gatsby, Daisy and Nick, the turning to illusion and "playing of roles" is part of an attempt "to recover the vibrancy and promise of their youth". There is something child-like about it, as Gatsby invents for himself a new identity of the sort "a seventeen-year-old boy would be likely to invent". Daisy's vision of what her life should be has its origins in her "white childhood", and it is this vision which leads her to marry Tom Buchanan, who can give her a $350,000 string of pearls; Nick returns to the Midwest where he felt safe as a child. As for Tom, a star football player in his youth: he was "one of those men who reach such an acute limited excellence at 21 that everything afterwards savours of anti-climax" (1). Nick sees him as child-like, someone who makes messes others have to clean up. But he once had a dream, too, though he has given up on it: he is "forever seeking, a little wistfully, for the dramatic turbulence of some irrecoverable football game". At the end, when saying goodbye to him, Nick feels suddenly "as though I were talking to a child".

Moments of hope and promise and wonder can be found only in the past, says Susan Parr. Despite this, "the conscious individual must nevertheless continue to hope and to struggle". This is the central paradox of the novel.

DRINK AND REMEMBRANCE OF TIMES PAST

Famously, Marcel Proust's passport into "time past" was a madeleine biscuit. In Fitzgerald's universe, it is booze. There is a telling description of the alcoholic Abe North (based on the alcoholic Ring Lardner) in *Tender is the Night* (Abe is in a Paris bar):

> A little later, with the exquisite manners of the alcoholic that are like the manners of a prisoner or a family servant, he said goodbye to an acquaintance... Afterwards, he just sat, happy to live in the past. The drink made past happy things contemporary with the present, as if they were still going on, contemporary even with the future as if they were about to happen again.

What would have happened to Jay Gatsby had he survived? He would, by the rules of Fitzgerald's universe, have become a lifelong drunk. Like his author.

Ten years after *The Great Gatsby*'s publication, in *The Crack-Up*, Fitzgerald wrote that one should "be able to see that things are hopeless and yet be determined to make them otherwise". We can at the same time be convinced "of the inevitability of failure" and still be determined to succeed. This was Fitzgerald's approach, says Parr,

> to the question of how the conscious individual comes to terms with the sense of hopelessness and human vulnerability that, in the case of *The Great Gatsby*, seems to be the product of an awareness of time's movement, on the one hand, and the belief that the modern world provides neither order nor meaning, on the other hand.

As this passage reminds us, Fitzgerald's novel was an attempt to come to terms, through fiction, with his *own* loss of youth and of illusions. The characters in *The Great Gatsby* are trapped, either by their dreams or by the lack of them. Gatsby doesn't *know* his dream is hopeless: he clings to it, and loses it slowly, painfully and, in the end, disastrously. Tom, on the other hand, who is aware he will never play football again, lost his illusions long ago, and their loss has made him bitter and unpleasant.

Fitzgerald is not trapped, like his characters, and can view them dispassionately. He *knows*

Gatsby's dream is hopeless. Swimming against despair, Fitzgerald has found a release, through fiction: the way to make something beautiful out of the mess of life is to write about it or make art out of it – the creation of tragedy as a recompense for loss. In this sense, art, though also only an illusion, is the only worthwhile illusion. "We have art in order not to perish of the truth," said Nietzsche.

Fitzgerald shared Conrad's bleak view of life, and also his view of the compensating power of art. Their views on the nature of human personality were similar, too. "If personality is an unbroken series of successful gestures, then there was something gorgeous about [Gatsby]," says Nick at the outset (1) and the novel endorses this view, or at least offers nothing to contradict it. In one of his letters, Conrad wrote about the difficulty of getting used to the idea that "one's own personality is only a ridiculous and aimless masquerade of something hopelessly unknown". Gatsby's masquerade is not aimless in his eyes – *he* believes in it – but it is a masquerade, and the novel reflects Fitzgerald's belief in what Marlow in *Lord Jim* calls "the essential sincerity of falsehood": the fact that man can have no more than a superficial, illusory solidity and that it is destructive to look beneath the surface. In an important moment, Daisy talks about how "everything's terrible anyhow... Everybody thinks

THE GREEN HAT

MICHAEL ARLEN

so – the most advanced people" (1), and proclaims the hope that her daughter will be "a fool" because "that's the best thing a girl can be in this world, a beautiful little fool". This reflects Daisy's own shallowness but it also reflects Fitzgerald's belief of how painful and difficult consciousness can be.

In *The Crack-Up*, Fitzgerald suggested that the best hope for the intelligent individual torn between the need to dream and reality was to try to function in the face of "the contradictions between the dead hand of the past and the high intentions of the future", and at the same time accept the contradiction inherent in doing so. Accepting this, he suggests, is the price of growing up, of losing youth.

The year before *The Great Gatsby* appeared saw the publication of another novel, *The Green Hat* by Michael Arlen, later made into a film starring Greta Garbo. *The Green Hat* is a much slighter story than *The Great Gatsby*, but it is also a story about the loss of youth (green being the colour of magic – and allure) and it also ends with a terrible car crash. In *The Green Hat*, the heroine, Iris Storm, though driving too fast, dies nobly – to protect other people – and while the society she moves in is condemned as worthless, she is not.

Fitzgerald had clearly read *The Green Hat*, but his novel is less comforting. There is nothing noble about Gatsby's death. *The Great Gatsby* is

opposite: the original cover of Michael Arlen's The Green Hat

not sentimental, like *The Green Hat*. Bleaker and more ambiguous than Arlen's novel, it raises questions about whether it is better to have illusions, false though they are, or to try to survive without them. Fitzgerald's attempt to rationalise his position in *The Crack-Up* – the idea that we must recognise the hopelessness of things while trying to make them otherwise – is not entirely convincing, but he would have agreed with Coleridge that perpetual cynicism is as naive as perpetual credulity.

In an interesting essay on Shakespeare's *Romeo and Juliet*, the critic Lloyd Davis sees *The Great Gatsby* as an important text in the history of love and desire in Western literature. Davis sees both Shakespeare's play and Fitzgerald's book as exploring the idea of desire as a "lost presence" – something which is based on nothing real but exists in the memory and most strongly when the desired is not present. Indeed Davis believes that *Romeo and Juliet* is the first major literary expression of this idea, an idea which Shakespeare, as it were, bequeathes to other, future writers:

> Though love continues to be celebrated as present or absent or present-in-absence in many texts (in different ways, Herbert's poetry and Bronte's *Wuthering Heights* come to mind), a significant line of literary works explores the interplay among desire,

death and selfhood. Like *Romeo and Juliet*, these texts place desire in conflict with time, recounting moments of ideal presence whose future reveals they could never have been. This revision of desire begins with Shakespeare's later tragedies – *Hamlet, Othello, Macbeth* and *Antony and Cleopatra* – where one lover survives, though briefly, to feel the other's loss. It runs from the fallen lovers of *Paradise Lost* ("we are one,/One flesh; to lose thee were to lose myself"), to the equivocal pairings at the end of Dickens's great novels or the images of foreclosed desire in Henry James's major phase.

The most poignant statement of desire as a "lost presence", says Davis, comes at the end of *The Great Gatsby*:

> *the green light, the orgastic future that year by year recedes before us. It eluded us then, but that's no matter – tomorrow we will run faster, stretch out our arms further... And one fine morning –*
>
> *So we beat on, boats against the current, borne back ceaselessly into the past. (9)*

If, looked at from this perspective, *Romeo and Juliet* can be seen as "the last tragedy of desire", later works like *The Great Gatsby* convey a different mood: "the note is of melancholic rather than tragic loss: what hurts is not that desire ends in death but that it ends before death".

How great is *The Great Gatsby*?

In 1990, Tony Tanner called *The Great Gatsby* "the most perfectly crafted work of fiction to have come out of America" and it undoubtedly has a power and a fascination which few short novels can match and which was underestimated by some early critics, like H.L. Mencken. While praising the charm and beauty of the writing in the novel, Mencken, whom Fitzgerald much admired, found the characters mere "marionettes" and the story itself "obviously unimportant". Fitzgerald, however, was quite capable, when the occasion demanded, of rounding out characters, as he does very effectively, for example, in his depiction of the tormented movie mogul, Monroe Stahr, in *The Last Tycoon*. *The Great Gatsby* is more impressionistic: he is dealing with a corrupt and superficial world and a world, moreover, in which what matters is appearance, where inner lives are more or less irrelevant – where the whole concept of an inner life is in effect almost denied.

It can be argued that in depth and richness of content, *The Great Gatsby* never quite matches the greatest works of the man Fitzgerald acknowledged to be his literary master, Joseph Conrad. Nor can *The Great Gatsby* really be compared with a novel as vast and complex as *Anna Karenina*, with its extraordinary insights into the love between men and women, a dimension missing in Fitzgerald's work as in much American fiction. It is not overstating the case to say, indeed, that many of the best American novels, like *The Catcher in the Rye* and *To Kill a Mockingbird*, are "buddy novels". There are exceptions – notably the unforgivably neglected Edith Wharton – but many of the great American writers, like Fitzgerald and his contemporary Ernest Hemingway, wrote essentially about relationships between men.

In a provocative essay in 1948, Leslie Fiedler ascribed this to what he called:

> the regressiveness... of American life, its implacable nostalgia for the infantile, at once wrongheaded and somehow admirable. The mythic America is boyhood – and who would dare to be startled to realise that two (and the two most popular, the two most *absorbed*, I think) of the handful of great books in our native heritage are customarily to be found, illustrated, on the shelves of the Children's Library.*

Moby Dick and *Huckleberry Finn*, of course, are

* Henry James, says Fiedler, can't be so easily categorised because he "stands so oddly between our traditions and the European ones we rejected or recast".

not just children's books, but *boys'* books – and boys' books which "proffer a chaste male love as the ultimate emotional experience".

Twelve years later, in his equally brave *Love and Death in the American Novel*, Fiedler says the essential difference between the American novel and its European prototypes is its "chary treatment" of women and sex – the subject *par excellence* of the novel being love or, more precisely, "seduction and marriage". Where, he wonders, is America's *Madame Bovary, Anna Karenina, Pride and Prejudice* or *Vanity Fair*?

> Perhaps the whole odd shape of American fiction arises simply (as simplifying Europeans are always quick to assure us) because there is no real sexuality in American life and therefore cannot very well be any in American art. What we cannot achieve in our relations with each other it would be vain to ask our writers to portray...

The endemic weakness Fiedler identifies, however – reflected in *The Great Gatsby*, essentially a buddy-buddy story about two men – is a weakness of the American novel as a whole. Putting it aside, how convincing, in its own terms, is the novel? How much does it really engage our sympathy? In a way, the strength of *The Great*

Gatsby is also its weakness. It takes a brutally deterministic view of its characters' lives: trapped in a society without morals, they don't have the capacity to develop as people or show any capacity for self-analysis. It is hard to escape the view that Fitzgerald disliked, even despised, them, including Gatsby. Most, with the exception of Tom, and possibly Jordan, lack energy; few of the interactions between them are engaging;

FITZGERALDIAN OVERWRITING

The Great Gatsby is sublimely well written. There are, however, moments in Fitzgerald's flights of prose which strike some readers as overwritten. Lines such as, "on that June night he came alive to me, delivered suddenly from the womb of his purposeless splendour" (4); or "his mind would never romp again like the mind of God" (6).

What does it mean that the hero, as we are told, has "drunk the Platonic milk of wonder" (6)? One can scent a distant allusion: in Coleridge's "Kubla Khan" and its enigmatic last lines:

> For he on honey-dew hath fed,
> And drunk the milk of Paradise.

Gatsby's West Egg mansion is planets away from Xanadu and the connections may be thought to be forced. When indulging in this overwriting, Fitzgerald gives hostages to some of his sterner critics. Most find – given the strategic placings of such passages – that they work. It was a constant issue between Fitzgerald and Hemingway: does fiction achieve its finest effects by economy (Hemingway's view) or by occasional extravagance of expression (Fitzgerald's view)?

they lack warmth and charm; their view of the world is too limited; were it not for the compelling way Nick tells the story, they would be of little interest. We don't feel, as we do in, say, George Eliot's *Middlemarch*, that this is a tragedy of unfulfilled potential.

In *Middlemarch*, both Lydgate and Dorothea marry worthless people: the former chooses a wife as he would a piece of furniture. (His choice is as shallow as Gatsby's dream of putting Daisy

---

HOW THE NOVEL WAS RECEIVED

Only the critic Gilbert Seldes identified Fitzgerald as one of the best living American writers. Fitzgerald was pleased by the praise of literary friends – H.L. Mencken, Edmund Wilson, and John Peale Bishop – and hoped that the novel would be a bestseller. After publication, he believed that the title – "only fair, rather bad than good" – the absence of an "important woman character", and the novel's brevity had damaged sales.

Only 23,870 copies were printed, in two editions in two printings in 1925; some were still in the warehouse when Fitzgerald died in 1940. The Armed Service Edition distributed 155,000 copies to military personnel.

Publishing history bears out his 1920 boast that he wrote for "the youth of his own generation, the critics of the next, and the schoolmasters of ever afterward". The reassessment of Fitzgerald occurred in the 1940s and 1960s and *The Great Gatsby* became a serious contender for "the great American novel". The book now sells more than half a million copies a year, with high schools and colleges

into his gilded palace or, for that matter, Citizen Kane's dream of doing the same to his "rosebud".) Lydgate's marriage to Rosamond and his decision, later, that he can't leave her, ruin his vocation and his life. Dorothea's choice of Casaubon is no less unreal: he, too, is worthless, as worthless as Daisy. But while Lydgate and Dorothea have dreams and ambitions that mean something, Gatsby does not. We believe in *them* in a way we never quite believe in *him*; Lydgate's loss seems

---

making up the biggest share of the market.

Hemingway wrote "It had a garish dust jacket and I remember being embarrassed by the violence, bad taste and slippery look of it. It looked like the book jacket for a book of bad science fiction. Scott told me not to be put off by it, that it had to do with a billboard along a highway in Long Island that was important in the story. He said he had liked the jacket and now he didn't like it."

For T.S. Eliot it "seems to me to be the first step that American fiction has taken since Henry James". The *New York World* entitled its review "F. Scott Fitzgerald's Latest a Dud": "*The Great Gatsby* is another one of the thousands of modern novels which must be approached with the point of view of the average tired person toward the movie-around-the-corner, a deadened intellect, a thankful resigning of attention, and an aftermath of wonder that such things are produced." For *The Chicago Daily Tribune,* "New Fitzgerald Book Proves He's Really a Writer". H.L. Mencken thought it "in form no more than a glorified anecdote". For Harvey Eagleton of *Dallas Morning News,* the book was "highly sensational, loud, blatant, ugly, pointless". Gilbert Seldes in *The Dial* was most complimentary:

greater, and more tragic, than Gatsby's.

That we are moved by Fitzgerald's novel is a tribute to the extraordinary power of his writing, to the beautiful imagery he uses and to his uncanny talent for creating a mood and capturing a particular world, so that we come to care about his elusive hero and to be saddened by his death. Yet there are questions which any intelligent reader must confront. Is there, for all its brilliance, a moral emptiness at the heart of the novel which vitiates

---

"Fitzgerald has more than matured; he has mastered his talents and gone soaring in a beautiful flight, leaving behind him everything dubious and tricky in his earlier work, and leaving even farther behind all the men of his own generation and most of his elders." Hemingway was critical, writing to Fitzgerald in 1929: "Nobody but Fairies ever writes Masterpieces or Masterpieces consciously – Anybody else can only write as well as they can going on the system that if this one when it's done isn't a Masterpiece maybe the next one will be. You'd have written two damned good books by now if it hadn't been for that Seldes review." On publication in England in 1926 the *TLS* was complimentary, but concluded that "it needs perhaps an excess of intensity to buoy up the really very unpleasant characters of this story". Edmund Wilson had commented in his letter: "The only bad feature of it is that the characters are mostly so unpleasant in themselves that the story becomes rather a bitter dose before one has finished with it." L.P. Hartley thought Fitzgerald's imagination was "febrile and his emotion over-strained... *The Great Gatsby* is evidently not a satire; but one would like to think that Mr Fitzgerald's heart is not in it, that it is a piece of mere naughtiness."

it? Surely Fitzgerald didn't feel that Gatsby should really be worshipping this worthless woman? Or is she perhaps the best that he can hope for given the world he's in? And is there really nothing else but such a world? If this is true – if this is Fitzgerald's vision – then does the book have the grandeur of tragedy? Does the loss of illusions itself constitute a form of tragedy, even if the illusions are not worth having? Or is this, rather, an anti-tragedy in that Gatsby's death is merciful since his worthless dream, like Emma Bovary's, is spared fulfilment? And is Fitzgerald as trapped by his own clear-eyed despair as his characters are by their dreams (necessary but hopeless – and doomed)?

These questions will go on troubling critics, and it is right that they should, but they arise only because *The Great Gatsby* is so clearly a masterpiece. The famous 20th-century critic F. R. Leavis believed that great novels were moral fables, to be read for their humane intelligence and moral maturity, and Lionel Trilling, the first to recognise the importance of *The Great Gatsby* in his book, *The Liberal Imagination*, argued, similarly, that literature was society's most potent civilising force and that a trained sensibility was the highest thing a civilised American could aspire to. Trilling thought *The Great Gatsby* lived up to this lofty view. He was right.

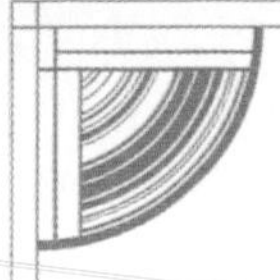

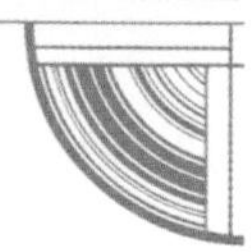

F. SCOTT FITZGERALD

A Brief Biography

Francis Scott Key Fitzgerald was born in 1896 in St Paul, Minnesota, the first surviving child of a wicker-furniture manufacturer. He was named in honour of a distant relative, Francis Scott Key, who wrote the American national anthem, *The Star-Spangled Banner*.

Both Scott's parents were Catholics. His father was from Maryland, old enough to remember the Civil War of the 1860s. Edward Fitzgerald imbued his son with the genteel values, and exquisite manners, of the "Old South". His mother was second-generation Irish, with "new money" (from the grocery-wholesale business) in her family background.

When Edward's business failed in 1898, the family moved to New York State, where he took up work as a salesman for the pharmaceutical firm, Procter and Gamble. When Edward was dismissed from that job, in 1908, the family moved back to St Paul, where Mollie Fitzgerald's inherited money saw them through. The sense of having been once wealthy and now "poor" scarred young Scott indelibly. Nonetheless the Fitzgeralds were well enough off to send him to a Catholic "prep" school in New Jersey.

Opposite: F. Scott Fitzgerald in 1936

He was already writing furiously and intending to make it his career.

In 1913 Fitzgerald entered Princeton University, with dreams of being either a star American football player or a writer of musicals. He neglected his studies and left Princeton, without graduating, in 1917, when America entered the First World War, to take a commission in the infantry. Expecting to die on the field of battle, Fitzgerald dashed off a novel (*The Romantic Egotist* – a self-revealing title) as his epitaph. He sent it off to the prestigious publisher, Scribner's, who rejected it but were not discouraging.

In 1918 Lieutenant Fitzgerald was posted to Montgomery, Alabama. Here, aged 22, he fell in love with an 18-year-old, golden-haired belle, Zelda Sayre, and she with him. Zelda was the daughter of an Alabama Supreme Court judge, who was not impressed by Fitzgerald. As Zelda's biographer, Nancy Milford, puts it:

> Fitzgerald was a charming and attractive but uncertain young man; he had not graduated from Princeton, he was Irish, he had no career to speak of, he drank too much, and he was a Catholic.

Despite this catalogue of faults, the couple became engaged, with the understanding that they would marry when Scott had the means to support Miss Sayre in the expensive style to which she was accustomed.

The war ended in November 1918, denying Fitzgerald the opportunity to win his spurs. On demobilisation he went off to New York, intending to make his fortune with his pen and marry Zelda. She, however, was unwilling to wait and broke off the engagement.

It was a bad time for Fitzgerald. Scribner's again rejected *The Romantic Egotist* but remained encouraging. Fitzgerald had better luck with short stories for the glossy magazines ("slicks"), which boomed in the postwar period. He would, over the course of his career, dash off 160 of them, and they were always a sure source of income. *The Great Gatsby* (which hovers, ambiguously, between novel and novella in length) draws on the author's early mastery of the short story form.

Finally, with the aid of Scribner's brilliant chief editor, Maxwell Perkins, (who also edited Hemingway) Fitzgerald came through with something publishable. *This Side of Paradise*, which drew heavily on the author's Princeton experience, was published in March 1920. It was an instant bestseller and Fitzgerald, at 24, was a literary celebrity. A week after the novel's publication, he and Zelda married.

The roaring twenties was a decade made for

Scott and Zelda. He was the laureate of the Jazz Age, and in many ways its icon. The camera loved him. Buoyed up by Scott's apparently inexhaustible literary earnings, the Fitzgeralds moved between fashionable resorts in Europe and America – including, significantly, a spell in Great Neck in 1922; West Egg in *The Great Gatsby*.

Fitzgerald's second novel, *The Beautiful and Damned* (1922) enjoyed similar success and reinforced the idea of "beautiful losers", to be found in all his mature work. But even at this early stage, Scott displayed the symptoms of alcoholism and Zelda early signs of her later dementia. Also evident was a growing artistic tension between the couple. As he went from success to success, Zelda failed, as a would-be ballet dancer and a novelist, to rival her husband's triumphs, and her behaviour became increasingly irrational.

In April 1924, the Fitzgeralds departed the hectic world of Prohibition America and settled in the French Riviera, where Scott set to work on his third novel, *The Great Gatsby*. Its composition, and Fitzgerald's marriage, were threatened by Zelda's falling in love with the French aviator Edouard Jozan. Despite the distraction, Fitzgerald, by now a consummate craftsman, completed the novel and *The Great Gatsby* was published in April 1925. A few weeks later, in

Paris, Fitzgerald met Ernest Hemingway – a novelist still to make his name. Their friendship would be close, complex, and brutally competitive. For Fitzgerald it would also be destructive.

The Great Gatsby did not enjoy the unequivocal success of its predecessors. Moreover, despite the large sums Scott was earning from his short stories and film rights, the Fitzgeralds were always broke. Money problems would afflict Fitzgerald for the rest of his life. The couple spent most of the next few years in France (the main setting for his fourth novel, *Tender is the Night*). Like other expatriate Americans, they were hit hard by the 1929 crash. The long Depression which followed made Fitzgerald seem, along with the Jazz Age he personified, historically irrelevant. When it was published, belatedly, in 1934, *Tender is the Night* registered a distinct slump in his appeal.

In 1930 Zelda suffered the first of a series of breakdowns. Despite cripplingly expensive psychiatric treatment, her condition worsened until she was permanently under professional care in the mid-1930s. The Fitzgerald's only daughter, Scottie, was largely looked after by friends (although Fitzgerald remained a solicitous father). His drinking was now out of control. This, the mid-1930s, was the period which he called "The Crack Up" – a phrase which would become the title for a posthumous collection of essays and such. Friends like Hemingway believed Fitzgerald would never write a good novel again unless he ditched his "nutty" wife, which Fitzgerald, true to his cradle Catholicism, resolutely declined to do.

In the last three years of his life, Fitzgerald (a "forgotten man", as he now thought himself) worked as a well-paid, but undistinguished, scriptwriter in Hollywood. He had no major screen credits to his name and his drinking led to his being regarded as unreliable by the studios. A vivid depiction of Fitzgerald in these last, wretched, years is given in Budd Schulberg's novel *The Disenchanted* (1950). There is also a rueful self-portrait in the Hollywood-hack, drink-sodden, comic hero of Fitzgerald's "Pat Hobby" stories.

His creative energy was not extinguished. Fitzgerald's Hollywood novel, *The Last Tycoon*, was only half finished at the time of his death, in December 1940. He died of a heart attack in the apartment of his mistress, the gossip columnist Sheilah Graham. Zelda survived until 1948, when she died in a fire at the hospital in which she had been confined.

WHAT THE CRITICS SAY...

F. Scott Fitzgerald's latest is a dud
[*The New York World*, 12 April 1925]

The first step that American fiction has taken since Henry James [T. S. Eliot, 1926]

My one complaint is that the basic story is somewhat trivial
[H. L. Mencken, 1925]

There is not a hole in it anywhere [Edmund Wilson, 1925]

It's not a matter of pretty writing or clear style. It's a kind of subdued magic, controlled and exquisite, the sort of thing you get from string quartets [Raymond Chandler, 1950]

I think my novel is about the best American novel ever written
[Fitzgerald to Maxwell Perkins, 1924]

Scott Fitzgerald has the one thing that a novelist needs: a truly seeing eye [Charles Jackson, 1935]

In The Great Gatsby *Fitzgerald adumbrated the coming tragedy of a nation grown decadent without achieving maturity* [Robert Ornstein, 1956]

A deep generating question behind the whole book is just this. As a result of the "domestication" of the great wild continent discovered by Columbus, what has been hatched from it?
[Tony Tanner, 1990]

The novel has a surface of uncharted depth
[Ronald Berman, 1996]

A SHORT CHRONOLOGY

1896, 24 September birth of Francis Scott Key Fitzgerald in Minnesota

1911, August writes his first play, *The Girl from Lazy J*

1913, September enters Princeton University

1917, 26 October receives commission as infantry 2nd Lieutenant

1918, July meets Zelda Sayre

1918, August Scribners declines *The Romantic Egotist*

1919, February discharged from army

1920, 26 March first novel, *This Side of Paradise,* published

1920, 3 April marries Zelda Sayre

1921, 26 October birth of Scottie Fitzgerald

1922, 4 March *The Beautiful and Damned* published

1924, April Fitzgerald records in his ledger "starting novel", which will eventually become *The Great Gatsby*

1924, May the family goes to the French Riviera, basing themselves at Cannes (a vivid description of their lifestyle on the Riviera is given in the opening pages of *Tender is the Night)*

1924, September first draft of *The Great Gatsby* (not yet so called) is finished. Over the next month, Fitzgerald revises, corrects the text, and has the manuscript typed up. It is sent to Perkins in November, who responds with criticisms later in the month

1925, January – February Fitzgerald, now in Rome, makes corrections to the proofs. The final corrections are made at Capri, in March

1925, 10 April *The Great Gatsby* is published by Scribner's in America. The first British edition is published by Chatto and Windus in February 1926

1930, April – May Zelda Fitzgerald suffers her first emotional breakdown, and is hospitalised outside Paris

1934, 12 April *Tender is the Night* published

1940, 21 December F. Scott Fitzgerald dies of a heart attack in Hollywood

1941, 27 October *The Last Tycoon* is published

1948, 10 March Zelda Fitzgerald dies in a fire at Highland Hospital

1948, 17 March Zelda is buried with Fitzgerald

BIBLIOGRAPHY

Belsey, Catherine *Desire: Love Stories in Western Culture,* Oxford and Cambridge: Blackwell, 1994

Bruccoli, Matthew (ed.), *F. Scott Fitzerald's The Great Gatsby: A Literary Reference,* Carroll and Graf, 2000

Bruccoli, Matthew, *Some Sort of Epic Grandeur: The Life of F. Scott Fitzgerald* (2nd edition, revised), University of South Carolina Press, 2002

Bruccoli, Matthew, *New Essays on The Great Gatsby,* (including "The Idea of Order in West Egg" by Susan Resneck Parr), Cambridge University Press 1985

Bruccoli, Matthew (ed) and Duggan, Margaret (ed) *Correspondence of F. Scott Fitzgerald,* Random House, 1980

Bruffee, Kenneth *Elegiac Romance, Cultural Change and Loss of the Hero in Modern Fiction,* Cornell University Press, 1983

Davis, Lloyd, "'Death-marked love': Desire and Presence in Romeo and Juliet", *Shakespeare Survey* 49, Cambridge University Press, 1996

Fetterley, Judith, *The Resisting Reader, A Feminist Approach to American Fiction,* Indiana University Press, 1978

Fiedler, Leslie, "Come back to the raft ag'in, Huck Honey!" Published in the *Partisan Review,* June 1948

Fiedler, Leslie, *Love and Death in the American Novel,* Penguin, 1960

Fitzgerald, F. Scott, "Winter Dreams", *The Collected Short Stories of F. Scott Fitzgerald,* Penguin 2000

Fitzgerald, F. Scott, "The Rich Boy", *The Collected Short Stories of F. Scott Fitzgerald,* Penguin 2000

Fitzgerald, F. Scott, *The Crack-Up,* New Directions, 1945

Fitzgerald, F. Scott, *This Side of Paradise,* Scribner 1920

Mizener, Arthur, *F. Scott Fitzgerald – A Collection of Critical Essays,* New Jersey, 1963

Parkinson, Kathleen, *The Great Gatsby, Penguin Critical Studies,* Penguin 1987

Parkinson, Kathleen *The Great Gatsby Penguin Critical Editions,*
London 1988

Prugozi, R, *The Cambridge Companion to F. Scott Fitzgerald,* CUP, 2002

de Rougemont, Denis, *Passion and Society,* first published in France, 1939. English translation, Faber and Faber Limited, 1940

Tanner, Tony, *Introduction to the Penguin Modern Classics edition of The Great Gatsby,* 2000

INDEX

A
Accidents 85
America, entropic view of 84–85
American Dream 72–87
Arlen, Michael
 The Green Hat 100–102
Arnold, Matthew
 "Dover Beach" 73

B
Baker, Jordan
 Edith Cummings, as 55
 man, behaving like 90
 Nick, affair with 7, 31, 90, 94
Belasco 43
Belsey, Catherine 50–51
The Beautiful and The Damned 116
Bishop, John Peale 108
Booze 97, 117
Brahmins 58
Bruccoli, Matthew 12, 64, 81
Bruffee, Kenneth 19, 22, 27
Buchanan, Daisy 6
 actions post-accident 92–93
 failure of Gatsby 87
 flowers, association with 47–48
 Gatsby, previous engagement to 7
 Gatsby's dream of 45–54
 grand passion, as subject of 52
 morally reprehensible, being 91
 Myrtle, killing 9
 past 45
 precious metals, association with 48, 61
 reversion to type 62
 self-absorbed, being 62
 voice 45–46
 white, dressed in 47
 worthlessness 92–93
Buchanan, Tom
 actions post-accident 92–93
 brutish nature of 30
 character on whom based 55
 civilisation, view of 77–80
 fascist tract, reading 43
 Gatsby compared to 63, 68–72
 infidelities 6, 69
 morally worthless, being 72
 nature of 6, 68
 Nordic blood 80
 racist views 77–80
 showdown with Gatsby 8
 "sweeties" 6

C
Carraway, Nick
 conduct, concern with 23, 25
 hero-worship of Gatsby 23
 hollow man, as 33
 interior rules 31
 Jordan, affair with 7, 31, 90, 94
 living life vicariously 33–34
 narrator, as 6
 past, embracing 95
 relationships 28–29
 repressed homosexual, as 90
 shadow line, passing 11
 shortcomings, effect on trustworthiness as narrator 28–34
 spectator, as 28
 tidiness 31–32
 Tom bullying 30
 truth, embellishing 33
 unheroic nature of 17
 women, view of 91
Cheating 68
Civilisation, Tom's view of 77–80
Cody, Dan 7
Collins, William 64
Conrad, Joseph 11 24, 28

Heart of Darkness 22–23, 26, 40
hollowness of names, making play of 40
influence of 21–27
Lord Jim 23, 26, 70, 99
The Secret Agent 93
Coppola, Francis Ford 66
Cowley, Malcolm 18
The Crack-up 98, 101–102
Cugat, Francis 66
Cummings, Edith 55

D
D'Amico, Jack
Davis, Lloyd 102–103
de Rougement, Denis
Passion and Society 51–52, 91
Dickens, Charles
Our Mutual Friend 81–82
Dreams
compelling nature of 95
Gatsby's, of Daisy 45–54
hollowness of 95–96
nature of 94–104
Dreiser, Theodore
The American Tragedy 58–59

E
Eagleton, Harvey 109
East Egg
falsity of houses on 80
"old money", populated by 6, 76–77
Eckleburg, Dr T.J. 66, 83
Eliot, George
Middlemarch 108–109
Eliot, T.S, 58, 109
The Waste Land 29, 62, 65, 82–83

F
Farrow, Mia 66, 86
Faulkner, William 59
Fetterley, Judith
The Resisting Reader 87
Fiedler, Leslie 88, 105–106
Fitzgerald, F. Scott
bad spelling 67
biography of 112–118
bleak view of life 99
death of 118
drinking 97, 117
family portrait 57
Great Neck, house in 56
historical detail, inaccuracies 12–13
marriage 115
military career 78–79
money 58–59
overwriting 107
peers, popularity among 66–67
portrait 113
sex, not writing well about 88
time past, drink as passport to 97
Zelda, meeting 114
Fitzgerald, Zelda
breakdowns 117
death of 118
Jozan, affair with 116
marriage 115
Scott meeting 114
Flowers, characters named after 89

G
Gandal, Keith
The Pen and Gun: Hemingway, Fitzgerald, Faulkner and the Fiction of Mobilisation 79
Gatsby, Jay
accident, state of mind following 40
background 36–38
Cody's right hand man, as 7
contrived nature of 40
corrupt or criminal actions 23, 25, 68
Daisy's relationship with Tom, not coming to terms with 52
Daisy, doomed dream of 45–54
Daisy, previous engagement to 7
death of 9, 93

funeral 39
greatness 63
green light, belief in 50, 52–53
Jimmy Gatz, as 7, 36–38, 41–42
library 42–43
military career 76–77
mobster, as 47
Myrtle's death, taking blame for 9
mystery and intrigue, aura of 35
name, invention of 14
new identity, defining 36
officer, training as 8
plausibility 35–45
poor background 60–61
rumours as to 6
self-transformation 42
showdown with Tom 8
solitude 35, 38
Tom, compared to 63, 68–72
wardrobe 41
wealth, source of 7
Wolfshiem, working for 8
Graham, Sheilah 118
Grant, Madison 78
Great American Dream 4, 72–87
Great Gatsby, The
American Dream, and 72–87
casual violence in 70
critics, views of 119
England, publication in 64
films of 66
first reaction to 4
"Great", use of 63
greatness of 104–111
Heart of Darkness, echoes of 26
Jazz Age, set in 12–13
key quotes 44
length 64
loss of illusions, about 12
masterpiece, as 111
original cover 16, 65–66
plot, summary of 6–9
reception on publication 108–110
shaky chapters 25
short story, theme prefigured in 15
studies of 65
time, references to 18, 64–65
title 10–11, 18
young man's novel, as 10–11
Great War, effect of 14
Green light 50, 52–53, 96, 103

H
Hartley, L.P. 4
Hemingway, Ernest 14, 58, 109–110, 117–118
sex, writing about 88

J
James, Henry
Portrait of a Lady 29
Jazz Age 12–13
Joyce, James
Ulysses 65
Jozan, Edouard 116

K
Keats, John
"Ode to a Nightingale" 46–47
Kipling, Rudyard
"The Story of the Gadsbys" 14
Klipspringer 39

L
Lardner, Ring 55–56, 97
The Last Tycoon 104, 118
Lawrence, D.H. 4
Leavis, F.R. 111
Luhrman, Baz 66

M
Mannes, Marya 74
Melville, Herman
The Confidence Man 74
Mencken, H.L. 4, 104, 108
Mizener, Arthur 94
Money
corrupting influence of 55–62
Fitzgerald, and 58–59
new and old 6, 76

N
North, Abe 97